PENGUIN BOOKS

BBC BOOKS

# THE TERRIBLE TWOS

Sarah Kennedy, a former speech and drama teacher, made the move into television and radio. Her wide experience ranges from the Saturday-night hit show *Game for a Laugh* to programmes covering the arts, current affairs and travel; and from the wedding of the Duke and Duchess of York to the twenty-four-hour British Telethon. She is currently working with Dr Desmond Morris on the *Animal Country* series, which is now in its eighth year. Her awards include Female Personality of the Year, for ITV in 1982 and for the BBC in 1984; TV Woman of the Year, awarded by the Variety Club of Great Britain in 1984; and the 1995 Sony Breakfast Show Award for *Dawn Patrol*, her programme on BBC Radio Two.

Sarah Kennedy loves gardening, Shakespeare and cooking. Humour is a very important ingredient in her life and work. In 1995 the first edition of *The Terrible Twos* reached the top of the bestsellers' list, raising £100,000 for BBC's Children in Need.

# The Terrible Twos

*Compiled by*

SARAH KENNEDY

PENGUIN BOOKS
BBC BOOKS

PENGUIN BOOKS
BBC BOOKS

Published by the Penguin Group and BBC Worldwide Ltd
Penguin Books Ltd, 27 Wrights Lane, London W8 5TZ, England
Penguin Books USA Inc., 375 Hudson Street, New York, New York 10014, USA
Penguin Books Australia Ltd, Ringwood, Victoria, Australia
Penguin Books Canada Ltd, 10 Alcorn Avenue, Toronto, Ontario, Canada M4V 3B2
Penguin Books (NZ) Ltd, 182–190 Wairau Road, Auckland 10, New Zealand

Penguin Books Ltd, Registered Offices: Harmondsworth, Middlesex, England

First published by BBC Books, a division of BBC Worldwide Limited, 1994
This expanded edition published in Penguin Books 1995
10 9 8 7 6 5 4 3



Filmset by Datix International Limited, Bungay, Suffolk
Printed in England by Clays Ltd, St Ives plc
Set in 10.5/12.75 pt Monophoto Bembo



**A royalty of 7½ per cent of the retail price of this book will be paid to BBC CHILDREN IN NEED on every copy sold**

# Contents

# Preface

Thank you for making last year's *The Terrible Twos* such an extraordinary success. We surprised even ourselves – the £100,000 raised, so far, for BBC Children in Need is a *wonderful* sum!

Opening any newspaper, one realizes fairly quickly that there is an enormous amount wrong with our world. In contrast is the quiet majority of decent people who really care, especially about children who have not been handed a fair pack of cards.

I am sitting writing this in my dining-room, looking at a bright orange file, about a foot deep, containing new *Terrible Twos* reminiscences. They are superb, so Barbara Nash (the book's Project Editor) and I have decided to add many new tales to this Penguin paperback to work more magic for BBC Children in Need.

Thanks to you lot, who write to me every day at Radio Two, the following *Terrible Two* certainly does *not* apply to *my* situation:

> *Our son, four and a half years old, was always excited when the postman arrived to deliver the letters. After breakfast one day I had just popped into the bathroom when I heard his shouts of great excitement as he raced up the stairs, hollering:*

*'Mum . . . Mum . . .'*

*'What is it, Andrew?' I called. 'I won't be a minute.'*

*To which he burst in through the door, shouting: 'Mum, the post has just come, and there's* ***nothing*** *for you!'*

So, thank you, again, for the pleasure you have given me and all Radio Two's *Dawn Patrol* listeners. And a special thank you for the contribution you have made to BBC Children in Need by buying this copy of *The Terrible Twos.*

This year has been a wonderful year for me – the success of *The Terrible Twos*, and the winning of the Sony Radio Award for our early-morning programme. I am thrilled to follow these with this *new double-the-size* BBC Penguin edition of *The Terrible Twos.*

Finally, here to sign off, are two of the Dawn Patrollers' most recent 'favourites':

*I was on a First Aid course and, while we were being instructed on the use and misuse of plasters, the course tutor regaled us with the following story.*

*Johnnie (aged five) came out of the boys' toilets crying and holding his private parts.*

*Dinner Lady: 'What's the matter, Johnnie?'*

*Johnnie (in very pained voice): 'I caught my winkle in my zip.'*

*Dinner Lady (very sympathetically): 'Ah, never mind, love . . . Shall we put a plaster on it?'*

*Johnnie (still pained): 'No, it's all right, I got one.'*

*Dinner Lady (very surprised): 'Oh, did the teacher get it for you?'*

*Johnnie: 'No, I took it off my verruca.'*

And:

*My nephew Shawn, aged five, had not long started school. My sister Vicki had just picked him up and was waiting at the crowded bus stop.*

*'Mum,' he suddenly announced, 'I know what they call men who love each other.'*

*You can imagine the thoughts that flashed through her mind . . .*

*'Oh, yes . . .' she said bravely, looking nervously around the queue. 'What's that?'*

***'Christians,'** Shawn replied knowledgeably.*

I hope you enjoy the book as much as *I* have enjoyed receiving your letters.

Sarah Kennedy

## Embarrassment

Doing my first teaching practice back in the mid-thirties at a school called People's College, I set a composition exercise called 'Wintertime'. When marking the exercise, I came upon a 'beaut', and I quote:

'I don't like winter mornings and going to school in the cold, so that's why I get into bed with Mum and the lodger before I get up.'

*Spider Davis*

Granddaughter Louise was in a real 'paddy' and wouldn't sit at the dinner table to eat.

Andy, her dad, lost his patience and told her he had thrown her dinner in the bin.

'Get me my f . . . ing knife,' Louise screamed at the top of her voice.

Andy stopped dead in his tracks, wondering where she had heard such filthy language and how to deal with it. Then the penny suddenly dropped as he realized she was saying fork and knife.

We are now trying to get her to say knife and fork!

*Jill Cattle*

When I was training many years ago, the Queen visited Great Ormond Street Children's Hospital. There was a five-year-old girl on the ward – a real Cockney sparrer – who had been known to use some *very* naughty words. She, of course, was the one Her Majesty elected to go and have a few words with. After a long silence, during which we all held our breath, Glenda gave the Queen a haughty look and said accusingly:

'You've got an 'at on just like me mum.'

*Judy Ryland*

I have two children, Dominic and Katie. Dominic talked very early and non-stop – morning, noon and night. Katie, fifteen months his junior, didn't talk at all – except to say 'Yes' for a sweet or 'No' at bedtime – and we were getting rather anxious that she was going to be a 'non-talker'. However, I shall never forget her first complete sentence!

One cold winter's day, she came in from the garden with her nose running profusely all over her lip, surveyed the room full of visitors and said in a very loud, clear voice:

'Who wants to wipe my nose?'

*Mary Taylor*

When I was two and a half, my aunt was plucking my mother's eyebrows one day. I suddenly looked up at her and said: 'My Daddy doesn't like you,' to which she proceeded to pull out my mother's eyebrows at the rate of knots.

As this was the *second* eyebrow to be done, my mother walked around for a couple of weeks with a *very* strange lopsided look on her face.

My father really didn't like her, so it really was a case of 'not in front of the children'!

*Yvonne Challans*

Once on a coach trip, when my son was nearly five and very small for his age, I sat him on my knee.

Out of the blue, he announced loudly, 'If the man asks me how old I am, shall I say three?'

I shrivelled in my seat!

*Mrs G.A. Collins*

While being assessed for school, my grandson was asked:

'What is a bush?'

After a moment or two, he said:

'They have them in the park, and you go wee-wees behind them.'

*Mrs V.M. Hallett*

When my daughter Elisa was small, my friend Maureen was on her annual visit and, as a treat, we'd arranged to go out together to see a show and have a meal beforehand, leaving Daddy to babysit.

Elisa was about five or six and very 'into' Barbie dolls, with their ballgowns all glittering with sequins, etc.

She watched 'Auntie' Maureen getting ready in her smart wool dress, and said perplexed, 'Auntie Maureen, did you know Mummy and you were going out tonight?'

'Oh, yes, love,' said Maureen, 'Mummy booked the tickets for the show in advance.'

'Oh,' said Elisa sadly, 'then it's such a pity you didn't bring something decent to wear.'

*Valerie King*

Ken (*aged three*): 'On your marks, get set, f . . . off!'

Me (*aghast*): '*What*?'

Ken (*unperturbed*): 'That's how Michael [the big boy up the road] always starts our races!'

*Gloria Pay*

When my girlfriend, Amanda, was two, she was taken by her mother to a local hairdressing salon. Amanda's mother, Jane, was a regular visitor and very well known in this posh suburb of Glasgow. As this was the late 1960s, the salon had the classic row of 'dome' hairdriers where you could have a milky coffee, read *Woman's Own* and have your hair dried all at once (as well as catching up on the local gossip).

Anyway, just as Raymondo was escorting Mum to her dryer, Amanda tugged her pink bri-nylon cape and said she wanted to go to the toilet. To no avail, her mum tried to coax her into waiting until they got home. Eventually Raymondo, as Mum was such a good customer, offered the staff toilet in the back of the shop.

With an angry Mum smiling unconvincingly to one and all, Amanda was duly escorted briskly through the salon, into the toilet – tights down, pants down, skirt up, seat – when Amanda's voice piped up: 'Don't need any more, Mum.'

Steam came from Mum's ears – but pants up, tights up, skirt down, march back through to salon.

'Good girl, Amanda,' Raymondo greeted them on their return, 'feel better now?'

'Oh, I didn't go,' Amanda replied. 'But my mum did a big jobby!'

'I did not,' shrieked Mum. '*I didn't.*'

'You did.'

'*I didn't.*'

And so it went on, with Amanda's mortified mum scanning the staring faces of the other mums and stylists, knowing they were lapping up every moment.

No sweeties for Amanda on the way home, that day.

*Kevin Toner*

An insurance collector had been calling at my home every week for years, so he was more like a friend. But I had never before had to tell him I couldn't pay him.

Consequently, one week when I really was short of money, I was feeling extremely awkward at having to ask him if I could leave it till next week. Then, when he knocked on the door, I suddenly had a brainwave and ushered myself and my two little girls into the kitchen at the back of the house, shushing them and trying to make it look as if we were playing hide-and-seek. Eventually, after knocking three times, he went away.

The following week when he called, I opened the door to him with a cheery grin and a jolly 'Hallo'.

'Hallo,' he answered, 'I called last week, but you weren't in.'

Before I could reply, my daughter, aged four, chipped in, 'Yes, we were. We were hiding from you in the kitchen.'

*Margaret Lakeman*

A particular fault of my son's early letters was a tendency to miss out consonants, especially at the end of words such as 'they', writing it without a 'y' or 'your' without an 'r'.

His aunts in the country, who kept a farm, were not

therefore over-impressed with a thank-you letter that commenced with the solicitous enquiry, 'I hope you cows are all right.'

*Tony Dudmesh*

My two children, Ellen (now eighteen and working as an au pair in Bordeaux) and Robert (now sixteen and a student at Myerscough College in Preston), were then aged four and two respectively. They were at that dreadful age when every time I caught sight of them they had a finger up their nose.

One particular day I was awaiting a visitor on whom I wanted to make a good impression, so I had a serious talk with the children, saying I didn't want to see either of them indulging in this nasty habit again.

The visitor arrived as expected and, with a meaningful look at the children, I went into the kitchen to make coffee, leaving them to entertain our guest.

You can imagine my embarrassment when, on emerging from the kitchen, I was just in time to hear Ellen saying to the visitor: '. . . and if you need to pick your nose while you're here, you can do it upstairs.'

The guest politely replied that he had never had a similar offer before. I don't suppose he has had one since, either. He never called on us again!

*Linda Coop*

My wife and I took our grandchildren, Tony, nine, Gary, seven, and Joanne, aged four, to the local pantomime, which was *Jack and the Beanstalk*.

The actor playing the king was heavily made up, and came round the audience handing out crisps and speaking to the children. After he had passed us, our granddaughter, four-year-old Joanne, turned to her nanna and said in a loud voice:

'Nanna, is he a Puff?'

*Alan Williamson*

A teacher set her class an essay on the subject of 'Washday Monday'.

One child wrote: 'On Washday Monday my mother gets up early and looks out of the window. If it's a nice day she goes downstairs and gets on with the washing. If it's raining, she says, "Bugger it," and goes back to bed.'

*Connie MacKinnon*

When my middle son, Adam, was six I was expecting our third child and his headmaster's mother said, 'I hear Mummy is going to have another baby – would you like a brother or sister?'

Adam: 'A brother.'

Mrs S: 'And what about Mummy? What would she like?'

Adam: 'A girl.'

Mrs S: 'And what about Daddy? What would he like?'

Adam: 'Oh, he doesn't want a baby at all.'

*Liz Bidwell*

A woman and her four-year-old daughter were in a shop buying a few groceries and chatting to the shopkeeper, a somewhat elderly gentleman. They were discussing at some length the forthcoming marriage of one of the village girls.

Towards the end of the conversation, the shopkeeper leaned over the counter and spoke to the child.

'What about you? Are you going to get married when you grow up, Anne?' he asked.

'Yes,' replied Anne.

'Are you going to marry me?' asked the shopkeeper.

'No!' replied Anne.

'Why not?'

'Because,' said Anne, 'my Mummy says you're a dirty old man.'

*Tom Reynolds*

When she was about eighteen months old, my youngest granddaughter (now seven) was brought to see me in hospital by her two brothers. After sitting a while on my bed she got restive, so I said:

'Go and say goodbye to the other ladies.'

Somewhat unsteadily, she trotted from bed to bed, saying, '*Die*,' to each old lady.

I had forgotten she couldn't pronounce her 'Bs'!

*Lyn Hodgkins*

My mother ran a pilgrim hostel in Spain, where the guests came from many different countries. My children, aged three, four, five and seven, helped out in different ways when we stayed there. One day we were expecting three very devout German ladies for lunch, and eldest son Paddy (now twenty-eight) was at the door to tell Grandma when they arrived. Seeing them coming along the street, he duly called out:

'The Germans are coming.'

As they entered, youngest son Danny (now twenty-five) dashed from behind the serving counter, dropped to one knee and, with very loud 'ack-ack' noises, machine-gunned them all down with an imaginary automatic.

I cannot begin to describe my total mortification. Even to think about it all these years later makes me cringe. The elderly German ladies, however, were very sweet and charitable, and pretended not to see or understand.

*Judy Duffy*

At my younger son's christening, Graham, then aged 'two and a lot' (two and three-quarters actually), was feeling left out.

At the party afterwards he sidled up to an elderly maiden aunt and confided in a wonderful stage whisper, 'I've got new pants on and they're grown-up ones. They've got a hole to wee through, would you like to see?'

*Julie Grey*

Mavis had told her three-year-old daughter, Fiona, to be on her best behaviour when she visited one of her aunts, who was a stickler for good manners.

'Always say "please" and "thank you",' cautioned Mavis, 'and, whatever you do, always be polite.'

At lunch, the aunt enquired of Fiona:

'Can you manage the meat, or would you like me to help and cut it up for you?'

'No, thank you,' Fiona replied, 'I can manage on my own. We sometimes have meat as tough as this at home.'

*Roger Wilson*

Our eldest daughter Louise (now twenty-six years old) could always be relied upon to give us something to laugh about.

When she was two and a half years old, we had just moved to a new district. My husband suggested I try out the local hairdressers – you know the hushed, reverent sort. I primed Louise to be a good girl and instructed her not to touch anything in the salon. All seemed to be going well. I had my hair washed and we had got to the cutting stage. By this time, Louise was leaning nonchalantly against the chair watching the male stylist with awe, when, in a clear dulcet tone for all to hear, she suddenly said to me:

'When *are* you and Daddy going to get married?'

*Wendy Clifford*

Years ago, when our son Neil was about three, he got up one morning and announced that I was to be his 'Auntie' for the day. I went along with his idea and, after breakfast, we made our way to town.

As usual the bus was crowded, but this didn't deter him. All the way it was Auntie this and Auntie that – he just did not draw breath. Suddenly a lady in front of us turned and said:

'I bet you're glad he's not yours.'

Needless to say I did *not* enlighten her!

I might add that he is still 'rabbiting' on, having been a schoolmaster in Derbyshire for twenty-six years.

*Lynne Hartburn*

We were invited to Grandma's and Granddad's for Sunday tea. We were all sitting round the table when Grandma said to our very young daughter, Gillian:

'Would you like some baked custard pie?'

You can imagine my expression when Gillian politely replied:

'No, thank you, Grandma, it's got dirt on it.'

Personally, I like nutmeg.

*Madge Worsley*

Joanna, six, and Graham, four, were on a day-trip to London and had been perfect little angels coping with the train journey, the underground and one or two sights before the *big* thrill of the day, a visit to the Science and Natural History Museum. We were on the top floor when Graham urgently stated that he needed to go to the toilet.

With no time to lose, we ran the full length of the top floor and down a large staircase to the ground floor. By now Graham's face was reddening and his hands were clutching the obvious places, so on we sped as fast as a frantic Mum and two little ones could go, until we reached a large room and stood facing three occupied toilet doors. At this moment Graham gasped and covered his mouth with his hand. My heart sank as I awaited the inevitable 'accident'. What did he say?

'Mummy, we needn't have rushed. It wouldn't have mattered if I did have an accident.'

Puzzled, I asked why not.

'Because,' he said, 'I've got my *brown* underpants on.'

The whoop of laughter from the occupied toilets made me rush him into a newly vacated one to save the day.

*Jacqueline Cadman*

Near-friends of mine were having an extension built to their home and their three-year-old, Julia, was closely involved 'helping' the builders with her bucket and spade.

On Friday the foreman arrived with the workmen's wage-packets and Julia was mortified to find she had not been included, running into her mother with bottom lip a-quiver.

The following week the men got together, putting money in themselves, and organized a wage-packet for her, with her name on and complete with tax and national insurance contributions.

This time Julia was overjoyed – her very own wages – and she immediately demanded to be taken to the sweet shop to spend the money.

Despite the shop being crowded, the shopkeeper joined in the fun putting the change back in the wage-packet, and, as they were leaving, he asked:

'Will you be working again next week, Julia?'

'I'm not sure,' she replied in that piercing voice only children have. 'It depends if they deliver the f . . . ing bricks.'

*Jan Owens*

Eddie and I were married in 1946 and I gave birth to our second son, Steven, on our sixth wedding anniversary.

On his first day at school, Steven proudly announced to the class:

'I was born on Mummy's wedding day.'

*Maude Milliss*

My granddaughter Sarah, then aged three, was walking along the High Street with her parents. In front of them, a large Boxer dog was being taken for a walk by the owner.

My daughter couldn't understand why the child kept bending down, peering at the dog's hindquarters.

On being told to walk properly, she said in a loud clear voice, 'Doesn't that dog look like Daddy.'

*Margaret Hillier*

We spent our holiday last year at a very up-market hotel in Scotland, with our two young sons, aged three and five.

One morning at breakfast, my husband and the boys finished and left the dining-room before I did.

Ten minutes later the children reappeared, threading their way through tables of people sedately murmuring over their croissants.

When they were about twenty feet away from me, I asked, 'Where's Daddy?'

In bell-like tones the three-year-old replied, 'He's having a poo!'

I lost consciousness at this point.

*Kim Shore*

My wife was a non-drinker and non-smoker but, during the Christmas festivities at a friend's party, she made an exception to the rule and drank quite a few 'shorts', etc.

Three-year-old Astrid, tired of playing, went to sit on her mother's lap, but, once there, complained, 'Phew, Mummy, you smell of Daddy.'

*Tony Bowler*

We were at a family cocktail party and one of the family guests was Uncle Arthur, who had something of a reputation for being a rather heavy drinker.

The couple giving the party had a small daughter, aged about four, and, as a special treat, she was allowed to hand round the cocktail snacks.

After her Uncle Arthur had taken a handful of cheese-straws, the small child, being particularly perceptive, returned to her mother and announced in a voice that all could hear (as only a small child can do), 'Mummy, Uncle Arthur doesn't drink like a fish. He drinks like anyone else.'

*Chris Short*

While touring *en famille* round the Welsh countryside, there came a thoughtful voice from my middle child, Sarah Louise, on the back seat:

'You c'n always tell a bull.'

Pregnant pause while we all waited for the next bit . . .

''Cos,' triumphantly from the back seat, 'it hasn't got any toots.'

*Ianthe Leadbetter*

Our Sarah (now seven) came out with these two beauties when she was three.

She had a pair of green wellies, decorated with frogs,

known as her 'frog boots'. These were worn with a sou'wester. One day, preparing to go out in the rain, she donned her boots and, after looking around for a while, called out:

'I've got my frogging boots on, but can't find my frogging hat.'

It puzzled her why I almost choked laughing.

The second incident was when Sarah was being taken to a yuppie pub for a lemonade and crisps. On getting out of the car her father caught his finger on a twig of a tree and it bled badly. They entered the pub and, as Dad went to lift Sarah on to a stool, her voice cut clear across the assembled 'posh' crowd:

'Take your bleeding hand off me.'

If we could only have stopped laughing, we might have been able to explain to the shocked onlookers.

*Eve*

Early one morning before breakfast my wife was having a few words with our neighbour over the fence. After a few minutes, she remarked that she was about to take a bath.

'Why?' the neighbour's three-year-old son asked. 'Did you wet the bed, too?'

*Harry Mitchell*

My grandson, Simon, is five. At the school he attends they run a project where the children are asked to bring an item beginning with a certain letter and put it on the table.

Letter 'S' was finished and Simon was duly asked to take home his snake.

'Next week's letter,' the teacher said, 'is "W", but I hope no one brings a nasty worm for the table.'

Simon, unruffled, looked straight ahead and said:

'I *hope* no one chops off their willy and lays that on the table.'

Exit one very embarrassed mum!

*Margaret Pilgrim*

I had arranged to collect a neighbour's children, along with my own, when nursery school closed. As the children piled into the back of the car, one little girl said, 'Oh, Mrs Fey, your hair looks really lovely today.'

Before I could say a thing, my dear son leaned over the front seat where I was sitting, ready to drive off, and putting thumb and forefinger together, he yanked at the crown of my head, shouting gleefully, 'It's a wig.'

You can imagine my embarrassment as I sat there with my own hair plastered closely to my head, while the wig flew through the air!

*Valerie Fey*

My granddaughter was getting her three children ready for school when Ben aged four and a half, started to cry, saying he didn't want to go.

After several minutes of coaxing, his mam ended with, 'You like school, Ben, you know you do.'

'I know,' Ben answered, 'but it's that little girl with long plaits. She keeps loving me all the time.'

*Vida Saunders*

My son Ben (now nineteen) was five when we first came to Suffolk. That first summer we visited the 'gardens' of Bury St Edmunds, and every house we went to I gave Ben instructions to behave himself, not to touch anything or remove any plants.

After what for him was probably a long afternoon, we arrived at the last garden to be viewed. The house was set back off the road – a beautiful rural setting. As we approached the house there were two *very* 'county' ladies sitting in their director's chairs, wearing the usual canvas hat and shoes. We paid our money and I said to Ben, 'If you want to wait here while we go around the garden, you may.' Just then one of the two ladies, with perfect diction, said: 'Yes, that's fine, let him sit there on those steps,' which he did.

As we moved off to inspect the garden, we heard one of the ladies say to Ben in a truly English plummy voice:

'Would you like to come over here and see the fish in the pond?'

To which Ben retorted:

'No, thank you very much. My mum said she would kick my arse if I moved.'

I promise you, I had said nothing of the sort, but, worst of all, we had to pass those two ladies on the way out.

*Linda Shotbolt*

My youngest son, Ben (now a strapping seventeen-year-old), will probably plot my early demise for writing this letter.

He was three years old at the time and we lived next door to a family whose grandma used to visit at frequent intervals. Ben was (and still is) a sociable and articulate soul who quickly became firm friends with 'Grandma', and they would often go off together to walk her labrador.

At this time I used to bake all my own bread, cakes and biscuits. One afternoon while they were walking Ben began to inspect the dog's hindquarters.

'What's that?' he asked pointing at the dog's genitals.

'That's his penis,' 'Grandma' told him.

'Oh,' replied Ben, 'my mummy makes penis biscuits.'

It won't surprise you that, on her return, 'Grandma' nearly collapsed in hysteria when I offered her a cup of tea and a peanut biscuit!

On another occasion, in the doctor's surgery, Ben, now aged five, picked up a leaflet warning of the perils of alcohol.

'Hallo, Ben,' the doctor greeted us and, seeing the tightly clutched leaflet, added: 'Have you got a drinking problem?'

'No,' said Ben indignantly, 'but my father has.'

Aargh, children!

*Leslie Smith*

On our very first family package holiday abroad, there was a very large woman whose behaviour embarrassed all the Brits, and I gave her the nickname of 'Fatty Harbottle'.

One evening my small daughter Holly, then four years old, was on the balcony when I heard her in conversation with the woman, who was enquiring whether I might have a needle to lend her. Imagine our consternation when our daughter shouted to us:

'Fatty Harbottle wants to know . . .'

Even now I colour up when I remember.

*A. Taylor*

We threw a party to introduce our three grandchildren to friends, other relations and neighbours. The party was in full swing – buffet, everyone milling round – me showing off my lovely grandchildren.

Suddenly, in the midst of all the frivolity, a little voice cleared her throat and Victoria, standing in the centre of everyone, trying so hard to get attention, finally got it. Silence – complete – and then Victoria, with hand coyly over her mouth, said:

'Please excuse me, everyone, but I have to go to the bathroom because I think I am going to *fart*.'

*June Smith*

In 1960 I had to travel home from Germany with Douglas, who was just two, and Kevin, six weeks. My husband booked me to travel first class because we would be in the centre of the ship, have a smoother passage and, hopefully, I would get more assistance.

What a journey! Douglas got hyperactive and ever more filthy, while I got more and more harassed. Before docking I took us all off to the bathroom, endeavouring to make us more presentable for the grandparents. I can still picture the scene – me a very young, dishevelled mum with scruffy, dirty child (definitely *not* first-class material). In walked a *very* first-class lady – you know the sort, furs and pearls. She went into the loo.

'Mummy, what's the lady doing?' Douglas asked loudly.

'Shush, darling. Come here.'

'But, Mummy,' he kept on and on, 'why won't you tell me?'

Eventually he was reasonably presentable, so I started on myself when, horror of horrors, his little voice suddenly piped up:

'Mummy, the lady's doing a wee-wee.'

There he was, lying on his tummy on the floor, his head and shoulders under the door.

I fled, abandoning my toiletries.

*Pam Pearce*

Every two years I accompanied a party of fifty boys, aged between nine and eleven, to France for an Easter holiday. During a visit to the Palace of Versailles, our female guide stopped in front of a painting of King Louis. As usual, we were joined by lots of adult English-speaking 'hangers-on' eager to learn more. The guide was very good, drawing the children's attention to the painting and pointing out his wig, his frilly collar and cuffs, and so on, until she eventually came to his high-heeled shoes. In a very loud voice, so all present could hear, she announced:

'Children, he wore these high-heeled shoes because, as you say in your country, he was a short arse.'

You can imagine the evil grins on the faces of the boys, the deadpan looks of the teachers and the hysterics of the 'hangers-on'. I often wonder if anyone corrected her or if, like us, they left her in blissful ignorance.

*Mike Scott*

When my son (now thirty) was little, we travelled by bus regularly.

One day my husband came with us and a *very* beautiful woman got on.

'Isn't she attractive?' my hubby said.

A couple of days later, Son and I were on the bus when the woman got on again, and in *that* voice that every mother dreads, he said, 'Oh, look, Mum, it's that lady Daddy says is a TRACTOR.'

*Kath*

My sister-in-law was shopping in a supermarket with my young niece, Janine, sitting in the trolley. At the checkout my sister-in-law noticed a black lady behind them in the queue and was immediately concerned, with good reason in the event, what Janine's reaction would be on seeing a black person for the first time.

'Hallo, lady,' my niece said cheerily, 'you've got a lovely hat on.'

Her mother was delighted, but only for a few seconds.

'But you've got a *very dirty* face.'

*Beryl Mingham*

Our identical three-year-old twins, Andrew and Ross, were noted for their antics – especially dressing up and dancing. Family and friends were sitting chatting in the lounge – waiting for a dress rehearsal – when the door opened, and the boys danced into the lounge wrapped up in toilet rolls with tea towels on heads and what looked like sticks of dynamite that they were waving in each hand.

My face got redder and redder as they danced with glee and shouted to all assembled:

'Mummy sticks these up her bottom.'

You can guess what *they* were.

*Jean Boston*

Our friend Maxine takes a ballet class of three-year-olds and, as the occasional accident happens, she keeps a spare pair of pants at the ready.

Well, 'It' happened, and the spare pair was duly lent, with instructions to bring them back next lesson.

The next week a room full of mums and dads were dropping off their little darlings, when this one's little darling piped up in a loud voice, 'Daddy's brought your knickers back.'

Red-faced Maxine!

*Kathleen Lawton*

Many years ago my sister Pamela was getting ready for bed and was going to change into her night clothes while some guests were present. My mother told her that she should go into the other room to change as it was rude to get dressed in front of people.

About two weeks later some of my parents' friends were coming to dinner and arrived a little earlier than expected. My sister was asked to open the door to them and explain. She did so and, in a very loud voice, announced:

'Mummy and Daddy are in the bedroom being rude, but they have nearly finished and will not keep you waiting long.'

*Raymond Hagley*

When I was a young man (way back in 1952) I was servicing a lady's Hoover cleaner, watched closely by a small boy of about four. He suddenly asked me if I had ever been in prison. 'No,' I said. 'I haven't.' To which he promptly replied, 'My daddy has.'

At this point, his mother hastened to explain that her husband had been a prisoner-of-war!

*Peter Barnicott*

I work from home as a freelance PR consultant and on this occasion was trying to be extremely professional while discussing an important matter over the phone with one of my clients. Richard, aged two and a half, hobbled into the kitchen with trousers and pants around his ankles, clutching his favourite Dinky car:

Richard: 'Mummy . . . Mummy . . .'

Me (*mouthing at him*): 'Sssshh, I'm on the phone.'

Richard (*thrusting his Dinky toy at me*): 'Mummy . . . Mummy . . .'

Me (*grabbing Dinky toy to keep him quiet*): 'Ssshhh – phone!'

Richard: 'But Mummy – it fell in the *poo* . . .'

*Hilary Jauncey*

A couple of months ago we were at a local restaurant having Sunday lunch with my two-year-old daughter, Joanna, and her grandparents. The table next to us was made up of four couples and, as the meal progressed, the women got louder and louder. Half-way through Joanna stood up on her chair, turned round and, in a loud voice, said:

'*Be quiet.*'

I don't know who was more surprised, the next table or ours. Ever wished the ground could open up beneath you?

*Carolyn Hufton*

# Logic

My son and daughter-in-law are trying hard to bring up their family in a peaceful manner – it is not easy. They regularly tell the children, 'We fight with words not deeds.'

One day my grandson came home from his playgroup very indignant because one of the other children had hit him.

His mummy sympathized with him, but said, 'I hope you told him we fight with words not deeds.'

Very earnestly, my grandson replied, 'Yes, I did, Mummy . . . then I hit him.'

*Ann Hayden*

A few days ago, I had come to the end of a very busy day (you know the situation – running around all day, working, cooking, the school run, ironing) and was generally under a lot of pressure. Joanne, aged four, then knocked her juice over the carpet for the second time. While mopping it up, I was telling her off (as you do) and she stood there, with big tears on her cheeks. When I had finished ranting, her little voice said:

'Have you finished the cross?'

'What cross?' I snapped, half listening. 'What do you mean?'

'Have you finished your crossness?' Joanne sobbed. 'Because I'd really like to have a cuddle.'

I felt such a worm. Don't children have a way of making you feel awful!

*Julie Seabridge*

When my grandson John was seven, I gave him a diary. He filled in his name, address and phone number in the spaces provided, then, coming to 'Blood Group', asked me what his was.

I replied that I didn't know, but if he ever went to a hospital someone would use a needle to take a sample of his blood, and would certainly tell him.

Before I could say more, he interrupted me, saying, 'I'm not going to bother with any of that. I shall just put down Red.'

*Margaret Gaukroger*

I was on a First Aid course and, while we were being instructed on the use and misuse of plasters, the course tutor regaled us with the following story.

Johnnie (aged five) came out of the boys' toilets crying and holding his private parts.

Dinner Lady: 'What's the matter, Johnnie?'

Johnnie (*in a* very *pained voice*): 'I caught my winkle in my zip.'

Dinner Lady (*very sympathetically*) 'Ah, never mind, love . . . Shall we put a plaster on it?'

Johnnie (*still pained*): 'No, it's all right, I got one.'

Dinner Lady (*surprised*): 'Oh, did the teacher get it for you?'

Johnnie: 'No, I took it off my verruca.'

*Jean Robinson*

David, then only five, was with the family having lunch at a pub. His mother and I were discussing his teacher who, unfortunately, had just had a miscarriage.

David, listening to the pair of us talking, said, 'What's a miscarriage, Mum?'

Red-faced, his mother said in a low voice, 'It's when you lose a baby. Now eat your chips.'

He ate a chip with a thoughtful look on his face, then suddenly said in a loud voice, 'My dad must have had a miscarriage when he lost me in Bolton.'

*Chris and Avis Parr*

Jack, three years old at the time, is the son of my friends, Kay and Chris. After a very stressful day, Kay locked herself in the bathroom for a 'soak', leaving instructions that she was not to be disturbed. Very soon, however, came a timid knock on the door.

'Yes, who is it?' growled Kay, agitated.

'It's the little boy who can make his own drinks now,' came the reply.

She discovered anew – laughter overcomes most things.

*Sandy Milne*

My granddaughter Victoria is two and three-quarters. Last Monday, she had her first ballet lesson. There were

ten children in the class, all looking very pretty in their little leotards.

Teacher asked the children to pretend to hold up an open umbrella and dance around to the music.

Victoria never moved and when asked by teacher why she didn't take part she said, 'I don't need an umbrella – I pulled up my hood.'

*Mrs S. Price*

My grandson David, aged three, especially likes the story of *The Sleeping Beauty*, and likes to answer questions. So the conversation went like this.

Me: 'The Prince went up the stairs, and what happened next, David?'

David: 'He opened the door and tiptoed over to Sleeping Beauty.'

Me: 'And?'

David: 'He kissed her and she woke up.'

Me: 'What happened next?'

David: 'She went to the toilet.'

*Margaret Gratton*

One Sunday I was washing my car when a squeaky little voice piped up, 'Excuse me . . .'

I turned round and saw a young boy all of five years of age.

'Hallo,' I said. 'What can I do for you?'

'What's your name?' he replied.

'Stanley,' I answered. 'What's yours?'

'Jerry,' he said.

'That's a nice name,' I said, and carried on cleaning the car.

'Excuse me,' the squeaky voice piped up again, and, when I turned and faced him, he said, 'Can I be your mate?'

I said that I thought I might be a little old for him, and suggested he make friends with someone his own age.

He was somewhat crestfallen by this, and said, 'I

have only just moved in and I don't know anyone.'

I pondered, then said, 'I tell you what – until you find someone your own age – I'll be your mate.'

He thanked me and meandered off, and I thought that was that. How wrong one can be. Every Sunday morning the front-door bell would ring and, when my wife answered it, there would be Jerry saying: 'Is Stan coming out?'

So, whatever I was doing, I would take time out and go into the garden with him and have a chat. This went on for quite a while until, one Sunday morning, my wife once again opened the door, and there was Jerry with his usual, 'Is Stan coming out?'

On this occasion when my wife replied I was busy, he was crestfallen and said, 'What's he doing?'

My wife explained that I was decorating.

'Decorating,' he said absolutely aghast. 'Decorating! We don't decorate – we move.'

The following Sunday, he thanked me for being his friend, then informed me he had found someone his own age and wouldn't be calling again.

*Stan Budd*

Our son Rex (now twenty-five) used to follow me about like my shadow when he was about two years old. On this occasion, following a day out to a holiday camp, where he could play and we could have a drink, we returned home and he followed me up to the loo, as was his wont.

Watching with interest as I performed, and plainly

aware of the route that the beer had taken, and the fact that I could blow cigarette smoke through my nose, he said:

'Make the smoke come out of your tiddly, Dad.'

Can you fault the logic? It's no wonder he has now got his degree in computers.

*Mike Maudsley*

When Jenny (now nineteen and at Oxford) was about four years old, we were on our way to see Granny and Granddad, when her little voice piped up from the back car seat and enquired:

'Are we going on the golden road, Mummy?'

'The golden road, darling?' I said. 'I don't know what you mean.'

'You know,' she said. 'You go down to the big roundabout, and then you go on the golden road.'

I thought for a minute of the route, and suddenly realized she had confused Dual Carriageway with 'Jewel' Carriageway!

*Dee Walden-Hughes*

Our great-aunt came to stay and, while she was with us, our dear grandmother (who lived next door) passed away. Needless to say, there was much activity first thing in the morning – with people coming and going next door.

My young brother, five years old, realized something special was afoot and, in great excitement, dashed upstairs to my great-aunt who was still in bed and said:

'Come on, Auntie, quick, wake up, Nanna's dead, and it's your turn next.'

*Patricia Levett*

When my cousin's wife and two children were staying with me for a holiday we three adults decided to go out for a meal on the last evening. A good friend said she would stay and look after the two children, Paul and Sarah.

We left the babysitter a box of chocolates for her trouble and said goodbye. The children, seeing us leave, both started to cry and, trying to calm the situation, the babysitter offered them a chocolate.

'Mummy', Paul the eldest said, 'says we can't have sweets after we have cleaned our teeth.'

Sarah, on the other hand, instantly stopped crying and, making a grab for the biggest chocolate, said:

'Doesn't matter. Mummy is *not* here now.'

*Graham D. Staplehurst*

My grandson Matthew had been having trouble controlling his bowels, and my daughter had taken him to the doctor. When things cleared up, the doctor told her to stop the medication.

Over Christmas, he had an accident and my daughter told him off. He replied that she hadn't given him his medicine. When she told him the doctor said he didn't need it, he replied, 'Doctors don't know everything.'

There's no answer to that, is there?

*Ruth Wilkes*

Stephen, four at the time (now nine), was staying at Nanny's house during the summer and had made friends with neighbouring children. They all played happily together, but Stephen had discovered the dreaded 'F' word from the older brothers of his friends. Nanny *very much* disapproved of this and told him that this was *not* a word that *nice* children used, and that if he must swear he must say 'flipping'.

This he did quite happily and could be heard saying things like: 'Where are my *flipping* shoes?' or 'It's *flipping* raining and I can't go out to play.'

The following Saturday I took him to Windsor Safari Park and we had a lovely day. When we arrived home, Nanny asked what animals he had seen at the park.

'Well,' he said, 'we saw the dolphins and the monkeys, and the camels, and the flipping-ingos.'

Now, whenever I see flamingos, this little gem comes to mind.

*'Aunt Joyce'*

My son Gareth (I'm very proud to say) is a Welsh Rugby Union referee. When he first started to referee some of the more important games, some were televised.

I was sitting with my grandson Aled, watching Gareth, and afterwards I said, 'Wasn't it exciting watching Daddy on television. What did you think of it?'

'Oh, it was all right,' he replied, 'but I wish he would play nicely with the others instead of blowing that whistle and putting his hand in the air.'

*Joan Simmonds*

Josephine, who is twelve, suffers from cerebral palsy, which mainly affects her legs. But, as with many people with disabilities, she makes up for it with other talents. In her case, it is her language skills. She started talking at a very early age and has not stopped since – she even talks in her sleep.

When she was about four years old she asked if she could have her ears pierced. I replied that she was too young, but she could make her own mind up when she was sixteen. She then went on to tell me the names of all the children at school who had had their ears pierced, including some boys.

I replied I didn't care if *all* the school had had their ears pierced, she could not.

At this point she scrambled furiously off the bed and crawled across the bedroom. When she reached the door, she shouted:

'I *wish* I had a *young* mother. If I had a *young* mother she would let me have my ears pierced.'

I was thirty-two at the time!

*Marie Wallace*

My grandson was asking his mother what time of day he was born.

'One o'clock in the morning,' she told him.

'I hope I didn't wake you up,' he said.

*D. Dunston*

When my son Ralph (now thirty-one and a lecturer in law at the University of Nottingham) was two, he was like a bottle of 'pop'. He hurtled everywhere from dawn until dusk with me constantly trying to cope. One day, after a lecture from me, and having been put to bed early due to my utter exhaustion, a solemn-faced, angelic Ralph reappeared and announced:

'Mummy, I have folded a new leaf to turn over.'

I had obviously included blurb about 'turning over a new leaf' in my lecture!

*Maureen Jäger*

Gareth had been to London for the day, and his mother had bought him a toy policeman's helmet. He wore it very proudly on the train journey returning to Guildford. The carriage was packed with city commuters.

Gareth sat quietly for a long time, and then suddenly turned and addressed the bowler-hatted gent next to him, saying, 'I'm not really a policeman you know – underneath this helmet I'm just an ordinary person.'

*Roy Cole*

I had taken my son Jamie, aged nine months, to my aunt, who used to look after him and my friend's son Nicolas, aged two years, while we both went out to work. Jamie, at nine months, was at the 'goo-goo-ga-ga' stage of playing with his voice, while Nicolas, although quite articulate, was still firmly attached to his dummy.

Upon arrival at Auntie's one morning, Jamie greeted Nicolas with his usual burbling 'goo-goo-ga-ga'.

Nicolas eyed him quizzically, took out his dummy and enquired: 'Does he speak English?' and replaced his dummy.

I think he got his pomposity from his father's side of the family.

*Pat Hodgson*

When our youngest son, now thirty, was three, we took him to the cinema for the first time to see *Bambi*. We were explaining to him what was happening when Bambi's mother was shot.

'Oh, dear,' Dad said to Andrew, 'Bambi's mother has been shot.'

And, in a very loud voice to a hushed audience, Andrew replied:

'Well, she should have run faster.'

The distraught audience roared with laughter.

*Anne Busby*

While working as a midwife I delivered a baby in the morning at the mother's home and returned later for the evening visit.

I was greeted at the door by the two-year-old who said:

'Have you come to take it back again? We've had it all day.'

*Marjorie Davies*

My daughter had a doctor's appointment for a blood-pressure check, so asked little Louise to hurry up.

'We are going to the doctor,' she explained.

'Why?' Louise replied. 'Don't I feel very well?'

*Joan Langridge*

Each child was asked to learn a verse and recite it to proud mums.

When it was Steven's turn, he stood up and, in a well-rehearsed country-bumpkin accent, said:

'Little birdie in the sky, did a packet in my eye, damn good job pigs can't fly.'

My husband had been busy wickedly rehearsing him behind my back.

*Mary Bachini*

My daughter was just home with her new baby son, and the district nurse called.

The nurse looked at the baby and said, 'Isn't he like his daddy?'

'No he's not,' said Matthew, aged four, 'he hasn't got a moustache.'

*Janet McCumiskey*

I told John we were going shopping with a friend.

'Oh, no,' he said, 'not that Marks-Expensive shop – you always spend so long there.'

*Diane Miller*

One Sunday when my daughter Monique was coming up to four, we drove down to Littlehampton.

After forty-five miles of her repeatedly asking 'Are we there yet?', I pointed to a huge blue sign board and read out loud, 'Welcome to Littlehampton.'

There was a short pause.

'Did that sign really say that, Daddy?'

'Yes,' I said. 'Why?'

'How did they know we were coming?' she replied, mystified.

*Clive Kavanagh*

A little boy was sitting in a cardboard box pretending to drive madly, and accompanying himself with car-tyre screams as he belted across the room.

'You in your motor car, then?' asked my friend to the little one.

'No,' he said, staring at her as if she was mad, 'I'm in a box.'

*Val O'Grady*

Some years ago, my small daughter (four and a half years) had her first PE lesson at her new 'big' school.

She said she had enjoyed it and added reassuringly, 'It's all right, Mummy, I didn't let the boys see my knickers.'

'How did you manage that?' I replied.

'Well,' she answered. 'I took them off!'

*Julia Marshall*

As a would-be fattie constantly fighting the battle of the bulge my mother always took artificial sweeteners in tea and coffee.

While entertaining friends for coffee one morning, she produced the sugar bowl, which was duly passed round.

My little brother looked on in fascination as various people helped themselves and then proclaimed, 'My mum doesn't have sugar in her coffee – she has aspirins!'

*Caroline Cassells*

Roanne and Steven are my step-grandchildren. They were visiting, and the three of us were sitting in the garden. The conversation went like this:

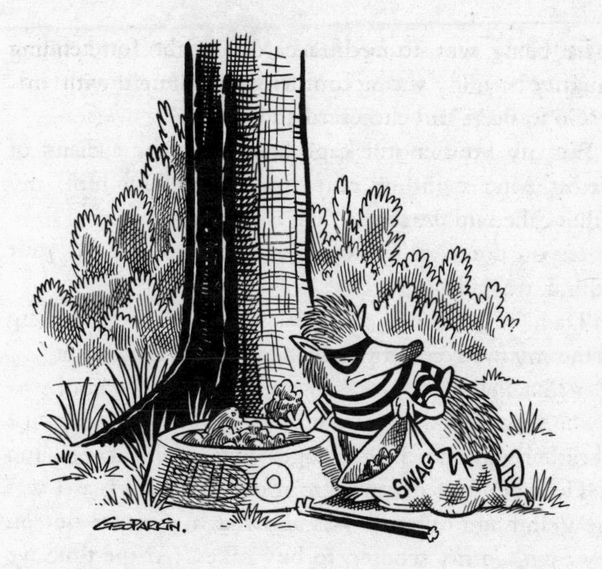


Roanne: 'Barbara, why have you got a dish of dog food in the garden under the trees?'

Me: 'It's there for my hedgehog. He likes dog food.'

Roanne: 'If we are very quiet, might we see him?'

Me: 'I don't think so, dear. He sleeps during the day and only wakes up at night.'

Knowing how progressive their parents are in their teachings, I thought they might know the word 'nocturnal', so I added, 'Do you know what we call someone who does that?'

Roanne: 'No, I don't.'

Steven: 'I do, Barbara. They are called burglars.'

*Barbara Godfrey*

After being sent to bed early one night for being a naughty boy, my young brother kept calling downstairs.

'Go to sleep,' my father called back.

But my brother still kept calling out for a drink of water. After eight or nine times of telling him, my father called up the stairs:

'If you don't go to sleep, I'll come up and tan your behind, my lad.'

'Dad,' my brother called back, 'when you come up to tan my bum, could you bring up a drink of water.'

*Sue Potter*

I was brought up in a village. The local baker's shop was a very short distance from our house and, as I was the grand age of six, I was allowed to venture out on my own, on my scooter, to buy cakes. (At the time we were eagerly awaiting the arrival of what was to become the first of my three brothers.)

On entering the shop, I was greeted by the baker's wife with what I heard as the familiar request:

'Hallo, and what will Mummy have?'

Confidently, I handed over the money for the cakes with the phrase I had learnt from my mother:

'Thank you, half-a-dozen fancies.'

This was greeted with peals of laughter. I had actually been asked, 'What has Mummy had?', meaning, of course, my expected brother.

Imagine my amazement when, thirty years later, married with two children of my own – and having returned to live in the area – I entered the same shop, to be asked:

'Half a dozen fancies today, then?'

On closer inspection I recognized a daughter of the owner's family. The story had been handed down. Fame at last!

*Jackie Bellamy*

My dear mum-in-law (who died just before Christmas) had a rather obvious wart on her nose, of which she was very self-conscious. I was busy reassuring her it was not as conspicuous as she thought and that she was far more aware of it than anyone else. Just then, in came Andy, aged four (now a plastic surgeon, funnily enough), and, gazing intently at Mam's nose, he said:

'Nanna, *when* are you going to pick that Rice Krispie off your nose?'

All my counselling was undone in a flash, but how we laughed.

*Gloria Pay*

A friend of mine took his young son to his first play, an amateur production of three acts. Each act was trying to prove that either education, religion or industry supported the world, but that, in the end, all three needed each other.

Finally the lead actor stepped forward and very solemnly put the following question to a quiet and thoughtful audience:

'Can you see it takes *all* three?'

'No,' was the very firm reply from a little boy in the front row.

This brought the house down, but the lead totally lost his composure.

*J. Beaton*

Our son Ian, who could swim, was playing in the pool with a polystyrene float. At one point, he slipped from this into the water, which was very cold.

An asthmatic, he lost his breath and, being then unable to shout, he was going under for the third time when he was spotted simultaneously by the life-guard and a friend who both dived into the pool to his rescue.

The lifeguard took Ian to the shower-room to get him warmed up.

Ian, no worse for his experience, was chatting away with him.

The lifeguard explained that he would normally provide people like Ian with a drink, but went on to say that because it was so early in the season he had no stock of drinks, so would Ian like a glass of water instead.

'Don't you think I've had enough water already,' Ian replied.

*Win and Neil Morley*

My daughters, Sarah and Catherine, are now aged nineteen and twenty-one. When Sarah was five years old she attended ballet classes held in a hall on convent land. One evening, Catherine, then aged three years old, came with me to collect Sarah after her lesson.

We were waiting in the car and, on this particular

evening, there were a number of Sisters walking around the grounds. Taken by their attire, Catherine wanted to know who these ladies were.

I explained very carefully that they were called Sisters or nuns, and that they had given up all their belongings – jewellery, clothes, everything – to live in the convent and work for God.

Catherine thought for a while and then said, 'Is that why they are called nuns, 'cause they haven't got none?'

*Janice Rolls*

Picture the scene . . . a very hot summer's day, a visitation to our street by the Water Board. The street was looking like a weird moonscape with its array of deep craters, as the workmen replaced our ageing mains supply.

My youngest daughter Amy (aged about nine at the time) came skipping up the street, clutching a bottle of pop. She stopped at the crater outside our house, and peered down into the hole at the workman below ground level.

'Would you like a cup of tea?' she asked.

The workman looked up hopefully, leaning on his shovel, as he wiped the sweat from his brow. With a great sigh, he replied, 'Aw, I'd *luv* a cup!'

'Tough!' my daughter replied with a really impish smile. 'The water's off!'

*Roy Garner*

David was at school and learning to read. He was at the stage where he read aloud everything in sight.

We were travelling to Scotland on holiday, and David and his younger sister were sitting in the back of the car. As usual, David was reading aloud the street names, etc. (not getting them all correct, I might add).

After a while, he said, 'Why are so many houses called "Bed and Breakfast"?'

*Margaret Slater*

A policeman, proceeding in a westerly direction, was passing by residential premises, when he heard the cry:

'Stick 'em up.'

Turning apprehensively, he saw a small figure, not more than five years old, in a three-cornered hat, a blanket for a cloak, a cap-gun in the shape of a flint-lock.

Correcting the young villain, he said:

'If you want to be a true highwayman, what you have to say is, "Stand and deliver – your money or your life."'

The boy's eyes narrowed, and his brow furrowed in thought, as the policeman continued on his beat.

Later that same day, as the policeman was proceeding in an easterly direction, the same cloaked figure leapt out from behind the front gatepost, shouting:

'Stick 'em up. Your money or your liver.'

*PC John Gisbey*

Two-and-a-half-year-old Grace was quite a character. Taken to children's service, she listened to the Vicar's address patiently for about six minutes, then stood on a pew and said in a loud voice, 'ENOUGH' (her new word).

She, like Mrs Thatcher, will go far!

*Pamela McCann*

Our neighbours' little boy James, aged two and a half, shouted from the kitchen, 'Mum, Mum, there's a rat in here.'

Mum, Caroline, rushed panic-stricken into the kitchen shouting, 'Where, where?'

'There,' said James, pointing.

It was an ANT.

*Rosemarie and Harry Rose*

When my younger sister and I were about three and four years old, an auntie came to stay with us from the Isle of Man.

My sister Dorothy was sitting on Auntie's knee, and she started pulling up Auntie's skirts.

Our mother scolded Dorothy and asked what she was doing.

'I am looking for her third leg,' she said.

She thought all Isle of Man people had three legs!

*Mildred Holding*

My small granddaughter, Chlöe, who lives in Warwickshire, was out with her parents last summer and saw, for the first time, a pond full of goldfish.

'Mummy,' she called excitedly, 'come and see all of these carrots.'

*Ann Thorne*

Gemma now eight, was only two and a half at the time of this incident, when she was refused something she had requested.

Her quick reply was, 'I *want* what I want, and I want it *now*.' Coming from such a tiny tot, this was really something. She will go far!

*Doreen Ralph*

When Daniel (now nine) was about six, we were listening to Radio Two when the record 'Walking my baby back home' was played.

Daniel listened and then said disapprovingly:

'Mum, I don't think that's very fair.'

'What isn't?' I asked.

'Well, that man's making his baby walk all the way

home and everyone knows babies can only crawl. He *doesn't* sound very nice.'

*Su Hillman*

Next door's children made a rare visit to our side of the fence. Invited inside, eight-year-old Jacob spotted our sheepskin rug lying on the floor – the animal shape with four legs and a head.

Studying it for a few moments, he asked:

'What animal did that used to be before it became a rug?'

'Well, a sheep or a lamb,' I told him.

His younger brother Jeremy, standing quietly beside him, pondered, then asked very suspiciously:

'What did you *feed* it on?'

On another occasion, Jacob and another of his brothers were running around with tablecloths attached to their shoulders.

'I'm Batman,' Jacob shouted to us.

As his brother came up, we said encouragingly: 'Who are you – Robin?'

'No,' he answered, hurt. 'I'm Thomas.'

*D.A. Bolton*

My twin nieces, who are two years old, have just got a video of Captain Hook. Towards the start of the video someone pours himself a glass of whisky. The conversation between Grandma and little Amy went as follows.

Amy: '*Silly* man.'

Grandma: 'Why is he a silly man?'

Amy: 'Because it will give him a headache.'

Grandma: 'How do you know that it will give him a headache?'

Amy: 'It *always* gives Daddy a headache.'

*Arthur Wyld*

On the plane returning from holiday Ben was staring out of the window. Suddenly, he said conversationally:

'I suppose some poor guy is sitting out there on the wing trying to spot the airports.'

*Sue Engel*

Grandma was taking her two grandchildren, Philip and Rosie, on a walk. Philip was walking and Rosie was in the pushchair. While feeding the ducks on a nearby pond, Philip noticed some horse manure (the area is used to exercise horses). As children do, he proceeded to ask Nanny some very awkward questions about the 'deposit'.

Nanny felt she had successfully navigated the difficulty, but unfortunately ended up by saying, 'And sometimes we collect it and throw it on our roses.'

On turning round she noticed Rosie crying her eyes out in the pushchair.

When asked what was wrong, Rosie said, 'You're not throwing *that* over me!'

*Joyce Crowther*

My next-door neighbour's friend had a young grandson staying with her overnight.

In the morning, she went into his bedroom, wearing a pretty pink négligé.

Child: 'Grandma, you look just like Madame Butterfly.'

Grandma (*preening*): 'Thank you, darling, but *how* do you know about her?'

Child: 'It's the name of our school pig.'

*Margaret Newton*

My grandson Christopher (then aged three) was having lunch with me near the dining-room window.

Suddenly a bumble-bee hit the window and flew off.

'What was that I nearly saw?' Christopher said, looking round.

*Pauline Nicholson*

When my daughter Lindsay was three (now twenty-five) she went into the lounge and put the TV on. I was

in the kitchen. She came running out to me and said, 'Mummy, there were these dogs racing on the TV and a rabbit got in with them, and he shouldn't have been there, and he won!'

*Jan Hodgkiss*

Sam came home from school one day and the following conversation took place.

Sam: 'Nana, do you know Sarah had a baby brother born last week.'

Nana: 'That's nice, darling.'

Sam: 'And did you know it was born three weeks early?'

Nana (*dusting away*): 'Really?'

Sam: 'Yes, and did you know they put it on an escalator.'

The mind boggles!

*Pat Brand*

Our son Tim, aged two, was in his pushchair, all muffled up against the cold, because the family were just setting off for a walk. As we did so we met an aged neighbour, also going on her constitutional.

'Hallo,' she said, bending down to greet Timothy.

After a moment's pause, he looked her sternly in the eye and said:

'You must *never* put your head in a plastic bag.'

Tim, now aged thirty-two and a Detective Sergeant in the Met, is still bossy.

*Tony Bondeswell*

Picture the scene: my then three-year-old-or-so daughter Rosemary (now twenty-three), a little blonde angel just out of the bath, all pink, sucking her thumb. I was in a bit of a mood, standing ironing, when this little voice said: 'Mummy, I love you.'

Suddenly, I felt life was worth living again and smiled at my sweet beloved child.

'So, when I am a big girl,' she proceeded to say (while I thought fondly what a delightful child to be so thoughtful), 'I'm going to get your face lifted.'

I laughed till I nearly dropped.

*Marlene Gillespie*

The recreation ground was completely deserted and my granddaughter, Louise, was happily tearing around on her tiny pedal tricycle.

After several circuits, she stopped by my wife again and announced:

'I'm going to let the others have a go now.'

After making a few more circuits of the area she stopped yet again, explaining breathlessly:

'I'm the others.'

*John Webster*

Paddy (now doing very complicated things with communication satellites and computers) showed remarkable resourcefulness in his early years. A quiet, thoughtful child, who enjoyed building with Lego, he was frequently aggravated by his younger brother tearing across the floor in his babywalker and smashing all his careful building work. He had been warned that he should *not* hit his little brother.

One day when I was on the telephone, I kept hearing shouts and roars of temper from little brother and the screams were increasing in volume. I went into the room to find the babywalker securely tied to the table leg by a skipping rope, and little brother walking round and round in ever-decreasing circles.

On another occasion, Paddy, infuriated by the antics of his younger brother's friends, invited them all to inspect the inside of the fruit cage and then simply dropped the latch and continued playing peacefully in the rest of the garden.

I can see why he now has a reputation at work for innovative solutions to problems.

*Judy Duffy*

My daughters, Susan, aged three, and Fiona, five (now in their twenties), were in the bath and their Dad and me were listening at the door. They were talking about what would happen if you had only one leg, when Susan said: 'You would just have to hop – for ever.'

*Anne Haines*

We have a caravan and on this occasion were taking our grandson, about four at the time, for a weekend. It was the first time he had been away from his parents on his own, and he wanted to sleep with my wife and me. He snuggled down between us and, after some chattering, all went quiet. We thought he had fallen asleep when, suddenly, a little voice piped up:

'Nanny, do moths have eyebrows?'

*N. P. Best*

When my eldest daughter, Catherine, was four (now ten) she came skipping into our lounge where my husband and I were sitting, and caught her foot somehow in the wheel of her baby sister's buggy and fell flat, hitting her head on the corner of a foot-stool.

On the twenty-minute journey to our local hospital, Catherine was lying horizontally across the car seat, and I was holding a compress to her head. I kept asking anxiously if she was feeling all right, to which she always replied, 'Yes.'

I then asked her if she could still see and she said, 'No.'

My heart somersaulted down to the pit of my stomach.

'Oh, my God, what can't you see?' I asked, fraught.

'The road,' came the calm reply.

*Allison Crimin*

My niece's little boy is five. I asked him what he'd like to be when he grew up. He thought for a few minutes and answered, 'A vet, but, before that, I am going to learn to swim so that I can take out the medicine to the fish when they are ill.'

*Peggy Kieser*

There had been a wax crayon lying on the side of the stairs for a few days, then suddenly there was a scribble on the grey gloss paint under it. Idly, I said to Lucy as I took her upstairs, 'I wonder who did that scribble there?'

'I don't know,' Lucy said. 'But if it was me, it wasn't my fault as there wasn't any paper there.'

*Sue Wells*

Some years ago I was down in Kent visiting my cousin and we went to Canterbury for the day, strolling around the cathedral with our children soaking in the history.

We suddenly heard a very loud whisper from her son Colin, who was around eight years old at the time and is now twenty-four. Speaking with a pronounced London accent, he said, 'Mum, Mum, come over 'ere and see where Becket copped it.'

He was standing at the spot where Thomas à Becket was gruesomely murdered!

*Mary Penney*

My four-year-old son early one morning:

'Mum, how long is a tube of toothpaste?'

Mum (*perplexed*): 'I don't really know, dear, as long as the tube, I suppose.'

Son: 'No, Mum, it goes all along your bedroom wall, then along the other ones.'

And it did!

*Geoff Poole*

Four-year-old Vicky (now aged six) was happily playing in the living-room while Mummy was busy in the kitchen.

On coming back into the living-room, Mummy noticed to her horror that her very wide nets had dramatically changed shape – and were now cut like 'Jardinière' in the middle.

On being asked why she had cut them, Vicky replied, 'So that my dollies can see out.'

Mummy, needless to say, was not amused!

*Doreen Ralph*

A friend and his wife arrived at their son's home for dinner and were greeted by their young grandson with:

'Guess what, Grandpa? We are having treacle tart for dinner.'

'Oh, that's wonderful!' Grandpa replied. 'So Mummy has been busy baking, has she?'

'Oh, Grandpa,' the little boy replied incredulously, 'don't be so *silly*. You don't *bake* treacle tarts. You *buy* them.'

*Geoffrey Coombs*

A friend had a young son who was always in trouble. For example, he would shut himself in rooms and then (at about three or four years old) would use a screw-driver – or whatever was available – to unscrew the door handles, locks and so on.

One morning, at four o'clock, his mother found him in the kitchen. There was a pound of bacon under the grill along with a pound of sausages, and six eggs broken into the frying pan.

'What are you doing?' she asked, amazed.

'Just getting you breakfast,' he replied.

*Sue Dyke*

My twelve-year-old youngest daughter, Claire, sauntered to the top of the garden where I was attacking the weeds – and *trying* to re-build our lives (my husband had been killed in an accident the month previously).

Claire: 'I'm bored. What can I do?'

Me: 'You could help me with the garden.'

Claire: 'I hate gardening.'

Me (*having thought for a moment*): 'You could clean the car for me.'

She sauntered back down the garden without saying a word. Five minutes later she sauntered back up to me, stood there for a moment and then said:

'I was going to clean the car for you, but it's *too* dirty.'

She's now twenty-four years old, presently in New Zealand, backpacking/working her way round the world.

*Audrey Davis*

When my son was between two and three we shared a house with the owner (we were a naval family on the move). One day the owner introduced my son to her stepfather, saying:

'Michael, this is my stepfather.'

A little time later Michael said:

'Has your ladder-daddy gone home?'

*Iris Hogben*

My four-year-old daughter, Helen, was listening to a conversation between my wife and me, during which my wife was telling me that her friend's son had returned home from college to inform his mother that he was *not* going to return to college but would 'take a year off' and . . .

Suddenly, my daughter raised her hands protectively to the side of her head, covered her ears, and uttered:

'He's *not* having *my* ears.'

My wife and I burst out laughing, but we now have a daughter who believes that there is a demented student on the loose chopping off ears. Two things in particular seem to worry her: how will she hear, and (even more important!) how will she be able to wear her sunglasses?

*David Howell*

Little Ben and I were spending the day together, and I said we were going out.

'Are we going to see that lady who loves me?' Ben asked.

'How do you know she loves you?' I asked.

'She calls me darling,' he replied.

*N. Crouch*

Lianne, about three, when he was taken to visit Tintern Abbey for the first time, looked up in awe at the beautiful old remains and remarked:

'Oh, isn't it beautiful – and won't it be nice when it's finished.'

*Norma Shreeve*

My great-niece Claire (aged seven) said:

'Auntie Christine, I had a horrible dream last night. A nasty man chased me down the stairs.'

Andrew, her brother (aged five), butted in (demonstrating with arm actions):

'And then I came along and punched that nasty man in his willy.'

Their dad is a police sergeant for the Met, so I am guessing that's what they've been advised to do!

*Christine Stockton*

My daughter Cheryl (now thirty-five) was three years old and her baby brother Michael about a year old. One morning I heard Michael cry out and, when I went into his bedroom, I found that Cheryl had smacked him.

'Why did you do that?' I asked. 'I can't believe you would smack your baby brother after telling me you wanted a baby brother and after me going to the trouble of getting one for you.'

'Well,' said Cheryl (hands on hips). 'Someone made a mistake 'cos that's *not* the one I wanted.'

What could I say to that?

*June Dixon*

Many years ago we had a small neighbour called John, aged three. This particular day he was offered a trip to Salisbury, which he accepted. As we swept down the hill off the downs, the cathedral was shining in the sunlight, the spire seeming to rise for ever and ever.

'How about sitting on top of that, John?' asked my husband.

There was dead silence for ages, then came the reply:

'No, thank you.'

'Why not?'

'It would make too big a hole in my bum.'

Thirty years on it still makes me smile.

*Jean Wiltshire*

Years ago, my sister took her small daughter, Anneva, out for a walk. They came across a funeral at the local parish church and questions were asked about the big box being carried into the church.

My sister explained as best she could – ending with the fact that the person was going to heaven to be with Jesus.

Later that day there was a rumble of thunder, and a little voice said, '*That* didn't take long.'

'What didn't take long?' my sister asked, puzzled.

'Well, for that man to get to heaven,' Anneva replied. 'I can hear Jesus opening the box.'

*Margaret Mann*

My son Alan was taking Thomas, my grandson, and myself to the coast for a day out. On the way, Thomas, in the child-seat at the back of the car, dropped off to sleep.

As we passed a field that was obviously having muck spread on it, I was prompted to comment to my son that the smell would not only bring tears to your eyes, but would put hairs on your chest.

I glanced behind to see if Thomas was all right. His eyes were closed, but he was grinning from ear to ear, shaking his head slowly from side to side.

'Somebody,' he said, 'has trumped, and it wasn't me.'

*Margaret Bennett*

One day while out walking with my two sons, someone came up to me and asked the way to the mill.

I gave directions and the person thanked me. As he turned to walk off, one of my sons said:

'I don't think people should go out if they don't know where they are going.'

*Valerie Hawkins*

When my daughter Catherine was about four years old, she stood in the bathroom watching me dress and said:

'Mummy, why do you wear *little* knickers and have a big botty, and I wear *big* knickers and have a little botty?'

Well, there was no answer to that then, and, today,

when I find myself squeezing into my underwear, I still think of this!

*Judi Morgan*

A daddy-longlegs was trapped in the house and I carefully explained how we must be sure not to damage its delicate legs as we tried to help it escape.

Clear blue eyes were turned to me in amazement: 'How do you know it's a daddy?'

I never did think of an answer.

*Joan Moeller*

Our four-year-old daughter was watching my wife struggle with the then-new-fangled bank cash-dispenser. She was quiet and thoughtful as the machine swallowed my wife's card, then took a step nearer as my wife pressed various keys and buttons and the machine began to whir. She looked expectantly at the machine as it pushed my wife's card back at her. Eventually, out came the cash and our daughter could not contain herself any longer.

'Oh, Mummy,' she cried, jumping up and down and clapping, 'you've won!'

*G. Johnson*

When my daughter was about six years old (now twenty-four and a teacher of English in a secondary school) we were out shopping as I had just acquired an Access card and wanted to see how easy it was to spend this new plastic money – too easy, I might add!

Driving home in the car I turned into a road, only to be confronted by a huge sign: 'Access only.'

'Oh, dear,' I said (very restrained, don't you think?), 'now we're in a mess.'

'No, Mummy,' said my daughter, 'we're okay because you have got your new card.'

Needless to say, every time we see an Access-only sign it brings back this memory.

*Wendy Hardman*

When our eldest daughter, Sarah (now in her mid-thirties), was about two and a half she absolutely loved bacon. One morning for no apparent reason she decided not to eat the bacon I had given her for breakfast. Trying to coax her, I said:

'Come on, Sarah, it's come from a little piggie.' *Mistake*!

With all the disdain a two-and-a-half-year-old can muster she said:

'I would rather have it from a shop.'

*Barbara Smith*

My daughter Lucie was just two when I first brought her brother Paul home from hospital.

We had been home for a few days and there had been a stream of friends and relatives to see us. Most of them had been very good about admiring Lucie as well, so that she wouldn't be too jealous, but one couple concentrated all their attention on Paul.

This was too much for Lucie, who stomped out into the garden, and, returning after a few minutes, said:

'Mummy, I've taken my knickers off, put them in a puddle and stamped on them.'

*Bridget Farrer*

I was sitting on a train with my young son, Benjamin. A couple of seats in front of us was a teenage punk rocker with orange hair, cut in Mohican style, which had been coiffeured vertically one foot above his head.

I could see that Ben was transfixed, and my worst dreads were realized when he said in a loud voice, 'Mummy, why does that man look like a chicken-birdie?'

*Mrs L.B. Brown*

I was walking my collie dog, Tam, on the beach when he suddenly ran ahead and lifted his leg in a pool of water near to the breakwater where a little boy was making sandcastles.

'James,' the boy's mother called urgently, 'come here.'

'Why?' James called back.

'Because,' his mother replied, 'that dog has just done a wee-wee.'

'So what,' James replied, 'so have I.'

*Jill Thornton*

This anecdote involves my niece Aimee, aged two.

It occurred when her mum and dad were defrosting the fridge, reaching that part of the process where the defrosted water runs all over the kitchen floor.

Aimee, who had just mastered the art of walking unaided and was enjoying the associated freedom, was pottering around downstairs in her playclothes.

A little while later, Mum and Dad, alerted by the noises and grunts that always accompany tinies who have just learned to manage stairs alone, turned round.

Aimee, having sized up the significance of the occasion, stood there in the kitchen doorway red-faced from her climbing efforts, and completely naked except for a pair of Wellington boots!

*Sylvia Mann*

I was stopped by my next-door neighbour, a shopkeeper, who mentioned that I owed him some money because my son had purchased some sweets. He then produced a bank paying-in slip covered in red crayon.

My son had written his first cheque at three, and it had bounced!

*Jack Dunbar*

Eileen, a friend of my mum, has a three-year-old son called Rhys. Like most mums she is 'soft' with him and rarely tells him off. On this particular day Eileen was late for work and my mum asked why.

Eileen replied: 'When I got up this morning I went into the kitchen only to find the floor flooded. So I had a look around and realized the fridge had been turned off. When Rhys came down I said: "Why did you switch off Mummy's fridge?" He replied: "I was cold, Mummy, and I thought that would warm me up."'

Rhys, bless him, had not been too well that week and had suffered from a hot-and-cold fever.

*Deborah Chalcraft*

Our sons Paul and Adam (now twenty and seventeen respectively) were both rather 'forward-thinking' and rather materialistic in their concerns for the future – in this life and the next – during their Terrible Twos phase.

At the time of his aunt's wedding, Paul, the eldest of the dynamic duo, was conscious of the material advantages of the occasion, saying to his young brother:

'Adam, when we're older, why don't we get married and then we'll get lots of presents.'

Then, concerns about whether you can take *it* with you started to feature in Adam's thinking from the tender age of three, although the precise location of the hereafter had obviously not quite registered.

'Mummy,' he said, 'when I die, will I go to Devon – and can I take my bike with me?'

*Nick Hills*

Andy, an only child, had a tremendous imagination when he was little and loved to live the part. He would watch Wimbledon with a towel over his head and *The Lone Ranger* with his home-made eye mask on.

Anyhow, after a few weeks of watching *The Lone Ranger* through the little slits of his black mask, he turned to his mum half-way through the programme and exclaimed:

'Oh, Mum, I shall be glad when this is finished so I can take this mask off.'

Two more for you! The very little girl next door used to come over the garden to see my mother and father-in-law and just sit and watch TV with them. One particular time after she had been there for about an hour, she turned to Margaret, my mother-in-law, and asked the time. She then gave a big sigh and said:

'Doesn't time go slow when you're bored.'

On another occasion when she was there, Margaret was in the kitchen rummaging through a drawer looking for something. The little girl, mesmerized by the contents of the over-full drawer, asked what was supposed to be in it?

Margaret said: 'Oh, this is just my rubbish drawer. Doesn't your mum have a rubbish drawer?'

The child looked horrified and said: '*No.* My mummy has a dustbin.'

*Caroline McClung*

This year, my friend's granddaughter, aged five, who lives in London, was to visit her grandmother on the Isle of Wight. Unfortunately, her visit was delayed by a few days and she missed the annual fireworks display at the end of Cowes week which she had been looking forward to.

A few days later, during a drive through the countryside, she suddenly said:

'Grandma, I know I've missed Cowes week, but when is sheep's week?'

*Tony Wadham*

Mummy, with fond memories of exhilarating crossings on ferry decks in her own childhood, dressed Oliver warmly – long vest (nappy, of course), long-sleeved woollen shirt, thick jumper and winter coat.

The weather was appalling – howling gale, lashing rain, freezing cold. There was no way we could be on deck, so we settled by a window in the warm saloon. Oliver, sitting opposite us, became redder and redder, and I said:

'He's far too hot, he'll be sick. Why don't you take his vest off?'

'If you think he needs it off,' she replied wearily, handing him to me, 'you take it off.'

With the boat rocking and bucking wildly and the

waves and rain hurtling against the window beside us, I laid him gently across my knee and proceeded to undress him.

Making a two-year-old's simple connection with previous experiences of being undressed in this position, he looked trustingly up into my face and said:

'No go swimming, Granny.'

*Beryl Slann*

Our son, four and a half years old, was always excited when the postman arrived to deliver the letters. After breakfast one day I had popped into the bathroom when I heard his shouts of great excitement as he raced up the stairs, hollering:

'Mum, Mum . . .'

'What is it, Andrew?' I called. 'I won't be a minute.'

To which he burst in through the door shouting:

'Mum, the post has just come, and there's *nothing* for you!'

*Margaret Wood*

A friend of mine, together with her daughter and three-year-old granddaughter, were walking round a well-known DIY store, with the intention of ordering a bathroom suite.

Suddenly her granddaughter had gone missing, and, after a frantic search, they found her, in full view of all the public, sitting on a display toilet with her knickers round her ankles, having a little light relief.

When a harassed male shop assistant explained to her

that this toilet was for display purposes only, she said: 'Go away. It's *very* rude to watch ladies on the toilet.'

*Jean Denney*

## Religion

Driving my four children to school/nursery/playgroup, Rebecca, aged about six at the time, suddenly said:

'Mummy, when's Jesus coming? I want to meet him.'

Me (*flippantly*): 'He's been and gone, dear.'

Rebecca: 'I don't understand – I want to meet him.'

Me: 'Well, you can't.'

Rebecca: 'Why can't I meet him?'

Me (*wearily*): 'Rebecca, Jesus was here one thousand, nine hundred and eighty-one years ago.'

Rebecca: 'Oh . . . Did you meet him?'

*Melanie Riches*

At about three years of age, Louise started to ask lots of questions about God and Jesus. I thought I had coped quite well with the probing questions, but, come the next day, breakfast over, out goes Louise into the garden to cycle round the paths on her Micky Mouse trike. As I was washing up the breakfast things and watching her through the window, she got off her bike, trotted up the path and said:

'Has God got a mummy?'

'No, dear,' I replied.

'Well, who feeds him?' she asked, puzzled.

'I expect Jesus's mummy does,' I said.

Down the garden she went and, two minutes later, appeared at the back door again asking for two biscuits, which I gave her. The next thing I saw was Louise breaking off little bits of biscuit and throwing them into the air, as high as her little arms could propel them.

'What are you doing?' I asked.

'Feeding God,' came the reply.

*Wendy Clifford*

My grandson Neil, aged six, exasperated with his sister Jenny, aged four, said: 'You think you know everything, Jenny, don't you?'

Jenny: 'Well, I do, then.'

Neil: 'Well, what is God made of then?'

Jenny: 'God is made of very strong metal.'

*Mr J.L. Taylor*

I have been enjoying reading a book of anecdotes about wartime evacuee children and I am sure the author, Ben Wicks, wouldn't mind if I relayed the following from his book, *No Time to Wave Goodbye*, concerning a foster mum recalling the six-year-old London girl they had adopted:

'Her first words were, "Who's the boss here, Auntie?", and being a bit taken aback I did not really know what to say, so I said, 'I am the boss of the house and Uncle (my husband) is boss of the garden,' to which she replied, "Well, God and me are boss of the lot."'

*Ewart Home*

I was spending a few weeks with my daughter, as she was expecting her third baby. On the second day of my visit, I collected Mathew, aged five, from school.

Mathew: 'Granny, I didn't think you would still be here.'

Granny: 'Oh, yes, I am still here.'

Mathew: 'Well, I have been learning all about God. When people get old he takes them.'

Then, looking up at me with a puzzled expression, he added:

'He *must* have forgotten you.'

*Mary Jones*

My mother died when my niece Jenny was a babe in arms, but she knows her Nanny Rose's house because it has been up for sale for a long time, and she regularly visits it with her daddy to keep the place maintained and the lawns cut. This is not Jenny's favourite outing because there is not much to amuse a two-year-old in an empty house.

Anyway, through playgroup, Jenny suddenly became aware that she did not have even one granddad, so she asked her mom why not.

Her mother told her that her granddads, like Nanny Rose, had gone to heaven.

Jenny put her hands on her hips and said, 'Oh no! Have we got to mow their lawns as well?'

*Liz Milnes*

My husband and I were having a special blessing service in church. We'd completed the Communion and the

Vicar was doing the Ritual Absolution. He lifted the cup, drained it, and my young nephew said in a loud whisper, for all to hear, 'Mum, he's drunk the bloody lot.'

*Liz Carruthers*

I have just had my two grandsons for half-term, to give my eldest daughter a chance to recover from pleurisy. They are nine and seven, and, oh boy, how my education is enhanced when they come to stay.

One suppertime, while chewing on my pork fricassee, I nearly choked to death when Richard, the eldest, said straight-faced:

'Do you know, Grandma, man's skin is so flexible that Nabob tied his ass to a tree and walked into Jerusalem.'

Then during 'afters', Daniel, not to be outdone, asked:

'Do you know who made the first ice-cream?'

'No,' I replied.

'I do, *I do*,' he cried triumphantly. 'It was Walls of Jericho.'

*Brenda Stone*

Our visiting minister said he had been taking a church service and had included for the children the hymn 'Jesus wants me for a sunbeam'. Looking at the congregation he noticed one small boy crying and being comforted by his mother. Later, the mother told him that her son had said, amidst tears:

'MUM, HE'S DRUNK THE BLOODY LOT.'

'Mummy, I *don't* want to be a "sunbeam for Jesus". I want to be an astronaut.'

*K.F. Ross*

I went to church yesterday, Mothering Sunday, and, as the children were going around giving the mums small posies of flowers, the Minister stopped one small boy and said:

'Now, where do you go when you want anything, and who do you go to?'

Expecting the small boy to reply, 'Mum,' the Minister and the rest of us were shaken when the answer came back, loud and clear, 'Sainsbury's.'

*Mary Fawson*

My granddaughter used to go to the Mums and Toddlers club held at the vicarage. The Vicar joined them for tea, so she was used to seeing him in his cassock.

The first time she was taken to church, on seeing the choir walk down the aisle, she called out gleefully:

'Oh, Mummy, look at all the little vicars.'

*Edna M. Webb*

My daughter, aged about seven, came home from school and asked, 'What is a prostitute?'

As quick as a flash my youngest daughter, aged about five, replied, 'You know, it's what dad is.'

Shocked silence followed, then I asked her what she meant.

'You know,' she replied, 'not a Catholic.'

*Bernadette Gray*

My son Alex was always a lively toddler and, in order to keep him quiet during the Sunday service, he was allowed a small toy car which he quietly 'brrr-brrmed' in and around the back pew.

The prayers continued and, at the point when the priest intoned, 'Now let us all join together and say the words the Lord has taught us . . . ,' his head shot up, the car flew from his hand and he shouted excitedly, 'What tortoise? Where's the tortoise, Mummy?'

*Lesley Polley*

My nephew Shawn, aged five (now twenty-seven, and father of Rhianne aged four months), had not long started school. My sister Vicki had just picked him up and was waiting at the crowded bus stop.

'Mum,' he suddenly announced, 'I know what they call men who love each other.'

You can imagine the thoughts that flashed through her mind . . .

'Oh, yes . . .' she said bravely, looking nervously around the queue, 'what's that?'

'*Christians*,' Shawn replied knowledgeably.

*Karen Margerison*

My father was a vicar so, even as a tot, I was familiar with the church and its graveyard, and with the various services that Dad performed: Holy Communion, Matins, Evensong, Weddings and Funerals.

Although I knew what happened at the first four, I wasn't so sure about funerals because I had never been to one. Mum did her best to explain, but, as she was soon to find out, I hadn't quite grasped the full significance of what she said.

We were travelling on the top deck of a bus, and the route took us past the church. As the bus drew up alongside the graveyard, the gravedigger, who had just finished digging a grave, was sitting on a nearby gravestone having a cup of tea from a thermos.

Mum could see I was deep in thought, then, after observing the gravedigger for a few moments, I turned to her and said:

'Mum, is that man waiting to be buried?'

*Michael Lewis*

My father sometimes collected Jo, five years old, from school in the car. On this particular occasion she hadn't eaten all her lunch and was finishing a sandwich. The conversation went like this:

Joanne: 'Daddy, is Jesus everywhere?'

Dad: 'Yes, love, everywhere.'

Joanne: 'Even in this car.'

Dad: 'Yes. He's everywhere.'

Joanne: 'Not in this sandwich?'

Dad (*emphasizing the point*): 'Yes. He is.'

Joanne (*after long pause*): 'Well, He'd better move over quick then when I take a bite!'

*Jaki Russell*

The following took place at the school dinner table where David was the question-master, and Kelly and Amy were the contestants in a quiz game.

David: 'This question is for both of you. The first one to give me the right answer is the winner. Who were the first people on earth?'

Kelly: 'Adam and Eve.'

Amy (*disgruntled*): 'It's not fair! I didn't watch that.'

*Diane, Ken and Polly Sturgess*

Me: 'What have you been up to this week?'

Thomas: 'I've been to church' (pram service for Mums and Toddlers).

Me: 'And what did you do?'

Thomas: 'Sang songs and played . . . and things.'

Me: 'What did you sing?'

Thomas: 'Achy Breaky Heart.'

*Paul Holcombe*

When my son was four he went to playschool in September and, just before this, we had to have our labrador put to sleep. I was so distraught I just couldn't tell him that Candy wouldn't be coming home again, so I said she was still at the vets' hospital.

At Christmas, I thought it would be a good time to tell him that Candy wouldn't be coming home, as she had 'gone to heaven to be with Jesus'.

Three weeks later his granddad died, and we said granddad had 'gone to heaven to be with Jesus to keep Candy company'.

At playschool, in March, the Vicar came along on St Patrick's Day and said: 'Jesus is here. Jesus is everywhere . . .'

At this point, Paul shot into the loos and locked himself in. They phoned me and, after some coaxing, he came out. When asked why he was so upset he said:

'Jesus has got my dog, he's got my granddad and now he's after me.'

Then, on Ascension Day, the Vicar held his hands high in the air and said: 'Jesus has gone back to heaven . . .'

At this point, Paul leaned over to me and said in a very loud whisper:

'Thank goodness for that! I never did like *her* anyway.'

*Diane Buckley*

A nearby clergyman preaching at the children's anniversary service, was stressing that the Bible is the best book – or the best book is the Bible. He then said to the children, 'Now, remember the three "Bs" – and if you meet me in the street I want you to be able to tell me that you've remembered my message.'

Lo and behold, a few days later, a little girl, about six years old, ran up to him in the street, saying, 'Oh, Vicar, Vicar, I can remember everything you told us last Sunday about those three WASPS.'

*Jean Dawson*

Many years ago, when my own children were small, there was a bad thunderstorm. The children were standing by the window, watching the rain.

There was an extra loud clap of thunder, and David said, 'I don't like thunder.'

'It won't hurt you,' his sister Maureen replied, 'but I'm afraid it will knock a hole in the sky, and Jesus will fall through.'

*Flo Edser*

The occasion was a birthday party in the early 1950s, when England was deemed to be a Christian land, and grace was said before meals.

Hence the mother of the 'Birthday Boy' was somewhat startled to hear a young guest addressing his devotions to Allah.

At a suitable juncture, she said to the child, 'You seemed to be praying to Allah – surely you meant God?'

'Oh, no,' he replied (expressing himself vehemently with all the scorn that his tender years could muster), 'I've finished with God. I pray to Allah now.'

It then emerged that he had lost his favourite marble and had asked God ever so many times to help him find it, but He didn't.

'I asked Allah only twice,' he added, 'and there it was.'

*Mike Trueman*

Being quite handy with a sewing needle I had made a Superman costume for a colleague's little boy, David (then aged about four), to wear to the local carnival. This went off very well and he even won a prize.

Just a few weeks later David came home from Sunday

school and reported that he had been chosen to be Jesus in a play. His mother immediately hunted out an old white sheet, and explained to David that she would ask me to make him a robe.

At this, David got *very* upset, stamped his feet and totally refused, saying he wanted to wear the Superman costume he had worn at the carnival. His parents pleaded with him during the next few days, but he remained adamant and got *very* upset each time any other item of clothing was suggested.

Finally, his Daddy sat him down and asked him *why* he thought he should wear the carnival costume. David's reply was very simple: the Sunday school teacher had told them that Jesus was a 'super man'!

They had to go out and buy an illustrated Bible before they could finally persuade David otherwise.

*Marcia Sims*

My granddaughter Stephanie was taken on an outing to the church near by.

Being a very chatty little girl, she said to the Vicar, 'My mummy and daddy got married here.'

'Yes,' said the Vicar, and then went on to tell the children, 'This is a special place. It's God's house. God is a very special person because He not only sees you all standing here, He can see right inside you.'

'My daddy is very special, too,' Stephanie chirped up. 'He can see right inside you as well.'

My son is a consultant surgeon.

*Margaret Fox*

Before my marriage I had attended chapel all my life but, since then, hadn't been near the place. The new Minister must have been gathering in some 'lost sheep' and decided to visit me at home.

My husband, who was a policeman at the time, working the late shift, was in the bathroom getting ready for work. As he was in the habit of floating about half-naked when he had finished, I asked my five-year-old daughter to go and warn daddy that the Minister had come to see me.

She obediently left the room, went to the bottom of the stairs and yelled: 'DADDY . . . THE PRIME MINISTER HAS COME TO SEE MUMMY.'

My husband entered the room with a very surprised and enquiring look on his face.

*Margaret Lakeman*

Before I became a teacher I was a church caretaker. One afternoon, alone in an empty church, I was polishing the floor. I looked up and saw a boy of about four years old gazing at me from the middle of the aisle. There was no one with him and I was about to say hallo, and ask where his mother was, when he turned and ran out.

Alarmed because the churchyard led straight on to a busy main road, I ran out after him.

I arrived just in time to hear his mother reprimanding him, saying, 'Don't you ever run away from me again!'

'But, Mummy,' replied the child, 'I only went inside

"... AND THEN 2000 YEARS AGO, YOU PROBABLY GOT INTO TERRIBLE TROUBLE FROM YOUR MUM FOR WALKING ON THE WATER WITHOUT YOUR WELLIES ...."

the church to see God, but he wasn't there . . . only his wife doing the work.'

*Joy Jeffrey*

Teacher to class: 'If Jesus walked into the room at this moment, what would you say to him?'

Little boy instantly: 'I would hand him the Bible and say, "This Is Your Life!"'

Who could he have been listening to?

*Pat Scott*

I have twin nephews, Paul and Craig, and, at the age of two, they used to attend Mass with me each Sunday morning. As I was Godparent to Paul (my other sister being Godparent to Craig) I decided to take my responsibilities seriously and teach them the 'Hail Mary' prayer. What better place to do this than during the Mass, where they would be able to become active participants and hear the prayer being said out loud. (It is not easy trying to occupy two-year-olds during Mass, and, more often than not, I would give them sweets to keep them quiet.)

To teach them the 'Hail Mary' I adopted the parrot-fashion style. The two boys were to repeat, after me, each sentence of the prayer; that is: 'Hail Mary' ('Hail Mary . . .' repeated by the boys). 'Full of grace' ('Full of grace . . .' repeated by the boys). 'The Lord is with Thee' (repeated by the boys). 'Blessed art Thou amongst women' (repeated by the boys). 'Blessed is the fruit . . .' ('Blessed is the *fruit pastille*,' the boys said).

Guess what they always ate during Mass! Now, each time I say this prayer, I think 'pastille', instead of: 'Blessed is the fruit of thy womb, Jesus.'

*Josie Duffy*

## Christmas

The following conversation took place between our eldest daughter and her four-and-a-half-year-old daughter, Bobbie, just before Christmas:

Mummy: 'Bobbie, do you think you are old enough to go to a pantomime?'

Bobbie: 'What's a pantomime?'

Mummy then went into a fairly simplified description of a pantomime, then asked:

'Well, what do you think?'

Bobbie gave the matter serious consideration, then looking at Mummy said:

'I would rather go to a Beer Festival.'

*Shirley Warman*

Just prior to Christmas last year we met socially with our friends and I enquired how their little 'bods' were doing. Santa Claus's lists were growing daily, they told me, but they were making sure Santa had noted the things on the lists *before* all the pre-Christmas advertising on television.

That day, however, the mother had seen an addition squeezed in part-way down the list, which was, most surprisingly, 'a pair of pants'. When enquiring why, youngest son Craig, aged five, having looked over both shoulders, whispered:

'Santa always brings me pants, so I thought I had better put them on the list.'

*Sandy Milne*

I was born and bred in Manchester seventy-seven years ago. After being in the Eighth Army in the desert for five years, my husband came home in 1946 and, in 1947, I had a baby girl. In 1952 my husband died of lung cancer, leaving me the widowed mother of a five-year-old girl.

Christmas was near and, as we only had each other, we went to my brother's on Christmas Eve, then had to walk two miles home. It was eleven p.m., the moon was shining brightly and a few snowflakes started to fall. My daughter, Jill, was tired and weary and I was trying hard to keep her happy, saying that Father Christmas would be arriving at our home soon and we must hurry. Just then, I saw a long ladder in a small garden reaching the roof and told Jill it was Santa's ladder and we must keep hurrying or we would miss him.

Suddenly, as we turned a corner, there *he* was (a man dressed up as Father Christmas). He, lovely man, joined in the deception and told my daughter that, because she had no daddy, he would treat her as *very* special and would be there very soon. She duly got her pillowcase full of small toys (some contributed by my large family) delivered by Father Christmas and was absolutely thrilled.

That made my lonely Christmas and, after that, my daughter always reassured her schoolfriends that Father Christmas was real.

She still talks of this Christmas at the age of forty-seven.

*Jessie Martin*

My sister went to a nativity play where the little Virgin Mary became exasperated with the little Lord Jesus and said fiercely: 'Stop your snivelling, Jesus.'

At another nativity, when asked, 'Is there any room at the inn?' the child replied, 'Oh, yes,' making the story of the stable quite redundant.

Finally, at yet another nativity, in answer to: 'And what shall the child be called?', the reply came back: 'Colin.'

*Olive Miles*

Our daughter-in-law is a teacher and the closing line of the school Christmas play brought the house down as a little boy (who had been *successful* until that moment!) said:

'Well, Father Christmas, I hope you and your elves have a sexfull night.'

*Doreen Fairhurst*

My granddaughter's classic! At Christmas '93 she was three and listening to my daughter Julie and me chatting in my kitchen just before Christmas Eve.

'How do you do your toast, Mum?' Julie asked innocently.

'Oh,' I replied, 'on the grill under the cooker.'

'You could do with a toaster, Mum.'

'Yes,' I replied. 'One day, when I've got a few pounds to spare, I'll buy one.'

'You don't need to save your money, Nanny,' my granddaughter piped up, 'Mummy has brought you one for Christmas. But you *mustn't* tell because *it's a secret*.'

Needless to say we fell about laughing, and now every time I do my toast I'm reminded of that and laugh.

*Jennifer Broughton*

Joe was a Terrible Two – all red hair and awful temper tantrums. For Christmas, when she was three and a half, she was given a doll's pram. Despite endless demonstrations she could not get the knack of folding and tucking the blankets under the mattress and became very cross that she could not achieve the result she wanted.

Grandad, witnessing this, sensed the temper building up and, seeking to defuse the situation, said:

'Well, let's see what we can do about this.'

Joe, very red-faced, replied crossly:

'Grandad, I shall *stamp* my foot and say *bugger*.'

We are *not* a family who swears, so goodness knows where she learned that, but it was so appropriate to her mood and temper that, even today, Grandad at eighty-nine is apt to say when something does not go quite right:

'I'll *stamp* my foot and say *bugger*.'

*Helen Brown*

As my dad was busy playing football (the nation's curse according to Mum) she decided to take us to see Father Christmas in a toy department. We got on the bus and, as it was nearly full, I was sent to an empty seat near the front while Mum and Steve sat on the long seat near the back entrance.

Opposite Mum and Steve sat a Rabbi, complete with long robes, silver hair and beard. Steve became more and more excited. Eventually he could not control himself any more and shouted to me at the front:

'Peter! Peter! *It's him* – it's Father Christmas!'

Poor Mum nearly died of embarrassment.

*Peter Harvey*

Nina was captivated with the story of the nativity, birth and eventual death of Jesus on the cross, and was overjoyed when she was chosen to be an angel in the nativity play. She learnt her lines to perfection.

However, Nina is given to adding her own logic to every situation.

The nativity was well under way and when it was her turn to say her lines to Mary, she said, 'Don't worry, Mary, you will have a lovely baby and you will call him Jesus.'

She then added, 'But I wouldn't get too attached to him, 'cos he'll be dead by Easter.'

*John Marshall*

When my youngest son, Neil, was just five and had been at school all of three months, he was, like lots of other children, learning Christmas carols.

On his return from school one day, he burst in with the news:

'Mummy, I know the name of the other reindeer. Do you?'

Well . . . I did my best with: 'Donner', 'Blitzen' . . .

'And *Olive*,' he said triumphantly.

Me, puzzled: 'No, darling, I don't think Olive was one of the reindeer.'

'Yes . . . Yes,' he insisted. 'The song says: "Olive the other reindeer used to laugh and call him names".'

After a stunned silence, the penny dropped. *All of the other . . .*

I laughed and laughed – Neil was not amused.

*Ann McKechnie*

When my son was three, I asked him what he wanted for Christmas.

'Just twelve brothers and sisters, please,' he answered.

Asked the same question, my niece Rebecca, aged four, said, 'Blackpudding and tomatoes on toast, please.'

Her brother Ben, then three, said, 'A rainbow.'

What are *you* going to ask Santa for this year?

*Lesley MacDonald*

Michael, aged six: 'Is Santa Claus *very, very* old?'

Mother (*dreading the moment of truth*): 'Yes, dear. He is *very* old. Why?'

Michael (*very thoughtful*): 'There will be hell to pay when he dies.'

*J. Munro*

My grandson Matthew, now six years, was unwrapping his Christmas presents under the watchful eye of his parents who were endeavouring to keep a measure of control.

Opening a parcel, Matthew groaned: 'Not a jigsaw puzzle.'

Encouraged to open the box, he saw the puzzle was complete.

'It's already done,' he said, greatly relieved. 'Good – what's next?'

'Not so fast,' said Dad.

So, the box was turned over and the puzzle broke into four large portions. Matthew promptly swept these four together and proudly proclaimed:

'There! That's it. Now what?'

*F. Brighty*

Steven, around six at the time, came home from school and told his mum and dad that he was going to be Joseph in the Christmas nativity play, and he had two lines to learn over the weekend.

Come Monday morning he was word-perfect, and went off to school in a very happy mood.

Alas, when he came home, he was crying, and it emerged that the teacher had told him that he could no longer be Joseph because his little friend was going to be Joseph, and he was going to be the inn-keeper instead.

From then on, the two little boys were enemies.

Come the evening of the nativity play all was going well – the school hall was packed to capacity, with the local Vicar as guest of honour.

When the part was reached where Mary and Joseph knocked on the inn-keeper's door and asked if there was any room at the inn, Steven came from around the scenery and boomed in his loudest voice, 'Yes, Mary can come in, but you can f . . . off.'

*Pauline Sullivan*

When my son Ian (now twenty-eight) was four years old, Grandma took him to see Father Christmas at the local store. He chatted away to Father Christmas and, when asked what he would like, explained at great length that he wanted a four-wheel bike, please, or two-wheeler with stabilizers.

'Well,' said Father Christmas, 'if you're a good boy, I'll see what I can do,' and he gave him a little gift (*too little* for Grandma!). She thought they should visit another shop to see if they could get Ian something better.

However, when the next Father Christmas asked Ian what he wanted, Ian placed his hands on his hips and declared in a very frustrated voice:

'Oh, no, not again – I've just told you down at the Co-op.'

*Pat Graham*

At three years of age, Ben was the youngest shepherd in the Sunday school nativity play. They were to wear tea-towel headdresses and dressing-gowns, but, as Ben had outgrown his dressing-gown, his mum adapted one of his dad's pyjama jackets for him to wear.

A few days later, on Christmas morning, Ben's face

lit up with pleasure when he pulled a new dressing-gown from one of his Christmas parcels.

'Look, Mum,' he called excitedly. 'It's a shepherd's outfit.'

*Joan Oughton*

The following conversation took place with my eldest son, Nick, when he was around five to six years old:

Nick: 'Jesus was born at Christmas time, wasn't he?'

Me: 'Yes.'

Nick: 'I was born at Christmas time, too, wasn't I?'

Me: 'Yes.'

Nick (*thoughtfully*): 'But he wasn't born the same year as me, was he?'

*Dianne Sims*

My little grandson, Jack, aged four, was in a nativity play, and was singing ('Just to practise, Nana'): 'The Wise Men in suspenders came.'

I looked at my daughter with raised eyebrows, but she, unable to help, shrugged, and neither of us said anything. He carried on singing very sweetly, and, suddenly, the second time around, I realized what he was supposed to be singing: 'The Wise Men in their splendour came.'

*Joy Palmer*

It was Christmas Eve, and my husband was watching the six o'clock news coverage of the riots and demonstrations that were taking place in Bethlehem. The pictures showed great gatherings of people on the streets.

On hearing the name Bethlehem, my son Andrew, aged seven, looked up from what he was doing.

'Is that Bethlehem, Dad?' he asked.

'Yes,' said my husband.

'What . . . Bethlehem where Jesus was born?' Andrew asked.

'Yes,' said my husband.

'Well,' Andrew replied, 'no wonder there was no room for Mary and Joseph at the inn – there are millions of them.'

*Caralyn Mintey*

My friend's little boy had watched his mother put up the Christmas tree and decorate the room.

'Come on, Connor,' she said, 'it's time for bed.'

'No thank you, Mummy,' he replied. 'I'm quite happy down here.'

Pure innocence, don't you think?

*Ann Blackford*

When my grandson, Felix, was six, he was to be St Joseph in the school nativity play. In the car on our way to see the play I asked if his friend, Harry, had a part.

'Yes,' said Felix, 'he's one of the kings.'

'Is he the one who takes the gold or the frankincense or the myrrh?' I asked.

There was a pause, then he turned to his mother and said suspiciously:

'How does Granny know this story? She hasn't seen the play yet.'

*Ann Bayley*

On a weekend visit, our five-year-old granddaughter, Mary, spent a lot of time rearranging the figures in our Christmas crib. When invited to admire the latest layout, my wife asked:

'Why is that wise man so far back from the others?'

'He's taking a photograph of the baby Jesus, Granny,' Mary replied.

*Peter Faulkner*

On the Sunday before Christmas my daughter and six-year-old granddaughter, Elizabeth, were to accompany me to the carol service at my church, where I was to read one of the lessons. As we got ready to go I explained to Elizabeth that there would be a short nativity play by the Sunday school children and carols sung by everyone.

'And,' I added, 'I shall be reading the Bible.'

'All of it?' she said with utter consternation.

*Joan Oughton*

## Easter

My son Jamie (now nineteen) came out, at the tender age of three and a half, with (to his mind) one of the most logical statements of all time.

I had bought him a large, fully illustrated children's Bible and he was lying on the floor looking through it, reading the odd words and making comments. Suddenly he reached the centre fold and cried out: 'Ugh – look!'

I looked down to see a very graphic picture of the Crucifixion: nailed hands and feet, blood and all. As gently as I could I explained how Jesus had been nailed to the Cross.

Jamie looked away, obviously thinking everything over. Eventually he looked up and said in a very serious tone:

'They could have used Sellotape.'

*Mrs J. Walker*

The sideboard was groaning with Easter eggs and presents, so my sister felt that she should tell her children the religious significance of Easter.

After lunch, Susan was wanting to get down from the table.

Mother: 'Say your grace, Susan, then you can leave the table.'

Susan: 'Not much good today – he's dead!'

*Collyn Freeland*

My son Andrew (now thirty-one) was five at the time, and we were discussing Lent and going without things to help people less fortunate than ourselves. You can imagine how proud I felt when Andrew announced that he was going to give up sweets for Lent, and send the money to the poor. Was this paragon of virtue really mine?

The first Sunday in Lent, as we were leaving church, Andrew asked to go into the sweet shop.

'But, darling, you've given up sweets for Lent,' I reminded him.

'I've decided to give up Brussels sprouts instead,' he replied.

*Mags Chue*

Just before Easter when my grandson, Matthew, was just four years old, I was explaining to him the religious significance of Good Friday and Easter.

'The chief priests and elders,' I said, 'had plotted to have Jesus put to death. They tied him up, beat him, made a crown out of thorns to put on his head, and made him carry his cross to the place where he was going to be killed. As he went by the crowd called him nasty names, spat at him and threw stones at him.'

At this point Matthew interrupted, looked me straight in the eye and solemnly asked:

'Nanny, did you throw anything?'

*Margaret M. Nicoll*

Our latest parish magazine revealed the following:

A young couple and their little daughter were taking an early spring weekend break in the countryside and, on Sunday morning, went to the nearby village church. The church was minus decoration during Lent, including flowers and organ music.

The four-year-old, puzzled by the unaccustomed silence, asked her mother, 'Why isn't the organ playing, Mummy?'

Heads turned in the congregation to see where the penetrating small voice had come from.

Mother, embarrassed, whispered hastily, 'Because it's Lent, dear,' upon which the same penetrating voice asked, 'Who to?'

*Bob*

The following comes from a young mother of our acquaintance.

Saul (yes, Saul) was playing and using last Easter's palm cross as a sword.

'We don't play with that because it's Jesus's cross,' his mother explained.

'Well, He's not using it, is He?' Saul muttered, walking grumpily off.

*Anita*

# Sex

A colleague, on playground duty, was confronted by an indignant boy, saying:

'Miss, Miss, he kicked me in the balls.'

Not completely sure she had heard correctly, my colleague said:

'I beg your pardon.'

Back came the response:

'Oh, you know, Miss, the tentacles.'

*Jean*

At the time of the Queen's Jubilee, my two sons were at junior and infant school. The elder one must have thought it was about time his younger brother knew a bit about the facts of life concerning the female body, and had obviously been telling him.

Come the day of the Jubilee they were having parties at school, after which the Headmistress read out a letter from the Queen signed Elizabeth Regina.

When Stewart, the youngest, returned from school, I enquired if he had had an enjoyable party.

'Yes,' he replied, 'but hasn't the Queen got a *very rude* name.'

*Barbara Rayner*

Happy to be a grandfather, I was looking after my grandson who was about two and a half at the time, and at the stage of struggling to stay dry all day. Not wanting to be bothered with changing wet clothing, I adopted the practice of taking Matthew to the loo every time I went.

On one of these trips upstairs, he used the loo first, then it was my turn. Mid-stream, he popped his head round my leg to get a full view, and said:

'My daddy has one of those.'

'Yes, that's right,' I said. 'All men have one.'

'Yes . . .' (Pregnant pause, followed by knowing nods from Matthew, followed by): '. . . but Daddy's is bigger.'

*Tony Austin*

We've always tried to talk about sex as frankly as possible and in line with our children's age and understanding. On a holiday in the Lakes we witnessed the rams 'running' with the ewes and had to get into more technical explanations and biological details to answer all Ben's questions. Ben took all this in his stride and seemed content with the explanation of the rams' and ewes' roles and no more was asked or said.

Several weeks later, different groups of family and friends coincided accidentally at our house and there was an air of polite friendliness between them as some of the more formal older relatives made conversation with some of our close friends whom they hadn't met before. Everyone was groping for common ground and, as often happens, Ben stepped in here.

Now, these friends, John and Jane, have no family, but Ben has long thought this ought to be changed. They were asking him about his holiday and he was giving them a good account of the mountains he'd climbed, the lakes he'd seen and, oh yes, the sheep in the fields:

'And . . .' he added for good measure, 'they were mating and now they're going to have lambs . . .'

Suddenly, going over to John and patronizingly placing his hand on his, he said:

'Why don't you and Jane make a baby, then we can all watch and see how it's done. All you have to do, John, is this . . . and then this . . .'

Amidst embarrassed coughs from older relatives and giggles (stifled) from others, one relative tried to save the day, saying:

'Ben, what a lovely jumper you're wearing! Did you get it for your birthday?'

*Sue Engel*

Man was just starting to explore space, and all manned rocket launches were televised to the world.

My son, aged about five or six, and I, were watching one such launch which was getting very close to lift-off.

Suddenly, he said, 'Dad, what's sex?'

For a moment, I was flabbergasted. I wasn't expecting such a question so soon. But I thought, Let's get it over with and find out what he wants to know. So I said to him, 'What exactly do you want to know?'

'Well,' he replied, 'it says on the screen four-minutes-ten-secs to lift-off. What's secs?'

*Mr G. Bishop*

Clare was about eight when she heard her mother's friend say that the birth of her youngest had been unexpected. Very interested in rabbits at the time (which might explain her reaction!) Clare blurted out:

'Why? Did your husband mate with you when you were eating or weren't looking?'

*David Sowter*

The following happened in the middle 1960s during the time of Green Shield stamps. It was around two in the afternoon and my mother had just waved goodbye to my father, who had been home for lunch, when she suddenly went into labour. By three p.m. she had given birth to my sister, Sarah. Our neighbour who had been at Mum's side throughout it all went home feeling very proud and satisfied with herself, only to be confronted by her young son, Peter, who asked:

'Has Auntie Audrey had her baby yet?'

'Yes,' she replied, 'it's a little girl.'

'Where did it come from then?' Peter asked.

Not wishing to go into the ins-and-outs, she replied:

'Oh, the nurse brought her in a Tesco's carrier bag.'

There was a long pause, then Peter suddenly said excitedly:

'Cor! Can I have the Green Shield stamps?'

*Wendy Lelean*

One sunny summer day a group of mums took their little tots to the beach, where they were all playing naked on the sand. The following was overheard:

Little Girl to Little Boy: 'Can I touch it?'

Little Boy to Little Girl: 'No, you've already broken yours off.'

*Retired Nanny*

"— I CAN SEE MY TESTICLES!"

Sitting in my car with my grandson (then three years old), waiting for Mum, he became bored.

Looking into the reverse mirror, he began to pull faces at himself.

Upon opening his mouth wide, he said: 'I can see my testicles.'

You try saying, without falling about laughing, 'No, darling, you mean your tonsils.'

*Anne Townsend*

My son-in-law, John, was sitting, legs spreadeagled, on the floor playing roll-a-ball with my two grandsons, Richard, then eight, and Aaron, then three. Aaron kicked the ball and, as it struck a very vulnerable place, John rolled round the floor in pain, with tears in his eyes.

'I'm sorry, Dad,' Aaron said. 'I'll rub it better.'

'*No*,' said Richard. 'You've hit him in the *nuts*.'

Whereupon, Aaron offered to kiss them better!

On another occasion, Richard, now aged nine, was explaining to Aaron that when mummies have babies they come out of something called a vagina. A moment later, he added:

'But if you can't say that word, you can call it a poppy.'

Stifling laughter, my daughter asked:

'Who told you that, darling?'

'Just at school,' was his nonchalant reply.

*Yvonne Reeves*

My eight-month-old granddaughter was taken to see her three boy cousins for the first time. When it was time for a nappy change, Rupert, aged five, showed great interest.

'She hasn't got a willie! *We've* all got willies. Why hasn't *Hannah* got a willie?' he asked.

'Don't worry,' Joseph, aged seven, piped up, ''spect she'll grow one.'

*Wyn Moreland*

My nephew Howard (now thirty-five) was not in the least worried about seeing the sex education film at school. His mother was a nurse and had always answered his questions truthfully, and he thought he knew all about 'it'.

What a different story when he came home from school, red in the face, having run all the way. He looked at his mother accusingly and said:

'You didn't tell me you had to take your clothes off.'

*Carole Salway*

I recently remarried and my young son, Richard, expected (as a matter of course) that I would have another baby. I gently explained that I had had six children (five grown up) and that I had all the children I wanted.

'It's not fair,' cried Richard, 'I want a baby brother or sister.'

I then explained that mummies only had a certain number of eggs in their bodies and all mine were used up. He accepted this. Later, he returned from school having had some sort of biology lesson.

'Mummy,' he said, 'boys are full of seeds, girls are full of eggs – and you, Mummy, are full of eggshells.'

Ouch!

*Sue Ovel*

Two girls, Melanie, ten years, Charlotte twelve, sitting directly behind me. Charlotte's reading, Melanie's doing nowt.

Melanie (*tentative voice*): 'Charlotte . . .'

Charlotte (*irritated at being disturbed*): 'What?'

'Do you know what a condom is?'

Charlotte (*same tone of voice*): 'Of course I do.'

Melanie: 'Well, what is a condom?'

Charlotte (*impatiently*): 'A condom is what Daddy puts on before he gets into bed in case he wets himself.'

*Jack E. Day*

Thirty-eight years ago, my daughter Christine suddenly said one day:

'Where did I come from?'

'Daddy and Mummy made you,' Mummy replied.

Long pause, then: 'Where did you get all the bits from?'

*Reg Man*

My daughter Frances (Fran), then about five years of age, had been particularly poorly one day with an ear-and-throat infection and, after a visit to the doctor's early-evening surgery, we went to the duty chemist to collect the doctor's prescription.

Sods' law decreed that we had to stand in the prescription queue next to the contraceptive counter and Fran asked in a loud voice:

'What are they, Dad?'

The smiles and grins of everyone encouraged her to continue asking until I felt that an honest answer was the only way out. I told her that they were contraceptives and that their purpose was to prevent Mummy having a baby.

Fran's show-stopping statement was: 'Well, I've *never* seen my mum eat any of those.'

The queue dissolved into helpless laughter.

*Patrick Conlan*

My son Andrew (now aged thirty-one) was three years old at the time this happened.

While being bathed, he looked down at his private bits and said, 'Mummy, is this my brains?'

As you can doubtless imagine Mummy fell about laughing and replied, 'I hope that's not where they are!'

My elder son, Tony, aged about five, came in and said, 'What are you laughing at, Mummy?'

I repeated what Andrew had said and Tony replied, 'Don't be silly, Mummy. He means his veins.'

*Ann Whittle*

Sadly, one of my colleagues was left as a one-parent family with a small boy, Craig, to bring up herself.

From a very early age he was continually asking leading questions, and despite being only twenty-something Mum held strong views that children should be children for as long as possible and was proud of her ability to neatly side-step the questions.

However, as time went by, matters deteriorated, especially when he started playschool.

One day he came home from school, bursting with the news that a classmate had had a new baby sister which had been brought in for inspection.

That night while Mum was bathing him, she decided that, against her better judgement, she had better tell him the Facts of Life.

She wove a story of which she was immensely proud, with a central theme of seeds and flowers in the garden, but including mummies and daddies and carefully using familiar words when naming the 'parts'. She told him everything: how the baby got in, how it grew and got out, and he sat in the bath absolutely transfixed.

She then lifted him out of the bath and, while she wrapped him in a towel, he asked:

'Mum? D'you have to take your jumper off?'

I understand she explained it was entirely optional!

*Jan Owens*

My eldest daughter, Karen (now twenty-nine), had suddenly at the age of three discovered those unmentionable parts of the male anatomy. I was coming from bathroom to bedroom completely starkers as was – and still is – my wont, when I was confronted by Karen. She looked, then trotted off to Mummy, saying:

'Mummy, what's that on Daddy?'

Mummy, deciding not to go into detailed anatomical explanations at this time, told her that it was Daddy's tail. We forgot about the incident until a few days later when we were visiting my parents. Karen, in deep conversation with my father, her granddad, suddenly asked:

'Papa, do you have a tail?'

Papa, of course, had no idea what she was talking about, but, putting it down to a little girl's chatter and fantasy, played along:

'Well, I did have one a long time ago,' he said, 'but I caught it in my bicycle chain while I was riding along and ripped it off.'

Karen accepted this explanation quite happily, but I always saw my father in a completely different light after that. There are some images that you just can't get out of your mind!

*Leslie Brock*

When my brother, aged two and a half, was in the bath with me one evening (I was aged four), he suddenly said to our mother – without any just cause or reason:

'If anyone ever asks me to be a daddy, I shall say NO!'

*Sue Reddish*

When Mark was about five or six he was playing in our back garden with our neighbour's little girl, Clare (about the same age). My wife and Clare's mother were in the kitchen having a chat and could hear what the children were saying and doing through the open window. Needless to say, they were particularly interested when they heard Mark say as he pedalled his go-kart around the lawn:

'Come on, Clare, let's play mothers and fathers.'

'How do you do that?' Clare asked.

'I drive, and you sit in the back seat and shout: "Don't drive so *bloody* fast!"'

*Anon*

My niece Nicky (now twenty-four) was staying with her grandparents and myself when she was three or four. When my father came home and gave mother a 'hallo' kiss, Nicky looked at me and, with her hand over her mouth, whispered:

'Oooooh, and they are *not even* in the bedroom.'

*Gillian M. Pratt*

Anna, my niece's daughter, aged four, was beginning to suspect that babies do not, in fact, come from under gooseberry bushes.

Anna: 'I don't want a baby.'

Understanding mother: 'You are not old enough to have a baby and, anyhow, your husband has to put a seed inside you.'

Anna (*after thinking for a while*): 'Then I shall keep my mouth shut.'

*Rosemary Waterman*

This story relates to Charlotte, who is now twenty-one, and a Prime Minister-in-waiting at the London School of Economics.

In 1976, when all the latest and best things were 'digital', Charlotte was taken to visit Father Christmas at the Co-op in Walsall. (By the way, it was September!)

Having been on the mystery sleigh ride, she stood at the old man's knee and pondered what she wanted for Christmas. After thinking long and hard, and going through the usual list of books and games, there was a pause. The cogs churned even harder.

'What I really would like is one of those Genital Watches,' she finally said.

*Graham Hicken*

When my daughter was aged four and a bit, our little Jack Russell, Coby, came into her first season. I told my daughter that, for the next two to three weeks, we *must* make absolutely certain that Coby stayed in and that the side gate was kept closed so that she could not leave the garden.

I then took this opportunity to explain what was happening to Coby and added that all ladies had something like this when they were grown up, and explained that I did and she would.

My daughter listened to all this with wide-eyed interest and then, after many moments of deep thought, she said, puzzled:

'I have never seen you stay in for three weeks.'

This misunderstanding reminded me of my own schooldays when I had been fitted out with a new uniform which included a green sports dress and knickers for PE. My mother called upstairs to ask me to throw down the green knickers as the elastic needed to be taken in. This I did, shouting anxiously:

'Mummy, please leave room for *gym*.'

It was some time before I realized what all the adult laughter was about – they had thought Jim!

*Mary Hunt*

While staying with my sister, husband and two young sons we decided to visit a garden centre. This was situated in the 'sticks', so we encountered some very uneven roads.

I was sat in the back of the car between the two lads. The youngest, then aged two and a half, urged his dad to go quicker. Wondering what the matter was, I asked him why.

'It's great when we go fast,' he said. 'It makes my winkle jump up and down when it's bumpy.'

*Claire M. Precious*

Many years ago when my nephew was four years old, his father, my brother, used to say to him after he had been to the toilet, 'Put it away, Victor, the ducks will have it.'

Well, they lived in a downstairs flat, and upstairs lived Gladys, aged three. This particular morning she came out on to the balcony with nothing on. Victor looked up and screamed, 'Dad, Dad, come quick, the ducks have had Gladys's.'

*Mrs C. Griffiths*

GEOPARKIN.

When my grandson, Daniel, was around four years old he was always taking off all his clothes and running around stark naked. So, I told him that, when he came to stay with us in North Wales, he would have to be very careful because there was a bird called a Willy Warbler that pecked off little boys' willies if it saw them.

Well, Daniel came to stay and we decided to have a day out at Portmeirion. After seeing all the sights, we settled down for a couple of hours on the lovely sandy beach. Before you could say 'Jack Robinson' Danny had taken off all his clothes. He soon found a friend and the conversation, overheard by the whole beach, went like this:

'Philip, my granddad says *that* bird there is a Willy Warbler and it will peck off my willy if it sees it . . . ' (wary eye and anxious pause) 'but it's not really, is it? It's a seagull.'

At this, all the people on the seashore fell about laughing.

*Graham Kinder*

My friend had twins, James and Suzy, who used to sit one at each end of the bath at bathtime. One evening James suddenly started to cry, quite bitterly. She asked him what was wrong, but he just continued to sob, so she lifted him out and, wrapping him in a towel, again asked what on earth was the matter.

James just pointed at his little sister and sobbed:

'I want a tucked-in one, like Suzy.'

*Dee Walden-Hughes*

# Pets

Two close friends have two daughters, Nicola (seven years old) and Carina (four years old).

Nicola had been given a hamster for her birthday, and a few weeks later her Mum noticed it wasn't looking too well.

Not wanting to upset Nicola, she took the hamster to the vet, taking Carina with her, while Nicola was at Brownies. Sadly, much to Carina's distress, accompanied by crying and wailing, the vet decided the kindest thing would be to put the hamster to sleep.

Within ten minutes of returning home, typical of children's reactions, Carina was as right as rain.

Mum then fetched Nicola, and decided to wait until they got home before gently telling her the sad news.

As they entered the house, perky-faced Carina rushed up to Nicola, saying excitedly, 'Guess what? Your hamster's DEAD!'

*Liz and Tom Newton*

My son Andrew was aged about four at the time of this story. We have quite a large garden and he used to love playing out in his pedal car. It was a lovely sunny day and I was doing my housework and checking on him from time to time.

All of a sudden there was an ominous silence.

I checked that the gate had not been opened and then called Andrew's name – nothing. I called again, a bit louder, and heard a muffled 'Mum'.

Following the direction of the sound I went up the garden. We have one of those green compost bins with a flip-top lid. I lifted it to find Andrew flat on his back, arms and legs in the air, and obviously unable to move.

Feeling like Joyce Grenfell, I asked, 'Andrew, what are you doing in there?'

'Sam pushed me,' was the reply.

Sam was our cat!

*Pam Bellis*

Alexander's younger brother Oliver (eleven months) follows him everywhere at a rapid crawl. Yesterday, Alexander was walking up and down the lounge with Oliver following close behind. My wife asked Alexander what he was doing.

'Oliver is my doggy,' he replied.

'What type of doggy?' my wife asked.

'A Yorkshire pudding, like Granddad Pooles's,' was the reply.

Granddad, of course, has a Yorkshire terrier.

*Robin Kent*

I have a new pup, a lovely golden retriever called Rosie, and I walk her daily in our country park.

Recently I had my two grandchildren with me, Jamie and Jennie, and, as we approached the only house in the park, there were four golden retrievers barking at the fence.

'That's where Rosie's dad lives,' I said to Jamie.

Very thoughtfully, he replied: 'Where does her mum live?'

'Oh, she lives in Macclesfield,' I said.

'Separated, are they?' Jamie asked.

*Joan Barton*

When my daughter was a baby we lived in a village in Cornwall. I had a pet bulldog named Annie, and my daughter and Annie were inseparable. I had potty-trained my daughter from an early age, so imagine my dismay when, at two years old, she stood looking out of the window, grunted and filled her knickers. Very cross, I took her to the outside toilet, sat her on the potty for five minutes and told her she was a 'dirty girl'.

After that episode, every day when the dog would 'do' what dogs 'do' in the garden, and the cows would 'do' likewise while being driven down the street for milking, she would chide all the animals and then say to me: –

'Dirty Annie, dirty moo-cows, no use Po-Po.'

*Helen N. Randall*

My niece told her son John, who was five years old, that the next day was their dog's birthday and he would be a year old.

'Are you going to make him a cake?' John asked.

His mother explained that dogs don't have birthday

cakes, but she would give him some extra dog chocs.
John thought about this for a minute and then said, 'Will lots of other dogs come to tea?'

*Elma Cherry*

Carol and Mom were standing at the bus stop with two small sons.

An elderly lady in the queue admired the two adorable little boys and enquired what they would like to be when they grew up.

Elder boy: 'I want to be a fireman.'
Younger boy: 'I want to be an Alsatian.'
*M. Gauntlett*

I was trying to warn my son Fergus, aged two and a half, that not all dogs are as friendly as our own dog, Luke (a springer spaniel with a heart of gold, who had been suffering silently while small hands, large toys, etc., were being stuffed into his mouth, and was still managing to smile weakly).

As I went on, I could tell that I was getting more and more bogged down in my explanation and, not wanting to confuse Fergus by telling him that Luke is a gun dog with a very soft mouth, I told him that Luke could carry birds and small animals, like rabbits, in his mouth without hurting them, whereas other dogs would probably bite them.

Fergus thought for a while, then said: 'Luke can carry little animals in his mouth, Mummy.'

Me: 'Yes.'

Fergus: 'He wouldn't carry a giraffe, would he?'

The vision of the dog with a giraffe between his teeth was too much, and at that point I gave up!

*Gabrielle Ewbank*

# Motorists

When our youngest daughter, Stephanie (now aged twenty-three), was small, we were out in our car, a much-battered Traveller, and in a great hurry to get from A to B. You know what it's like, whenever you're in a rush there's always something to slow you down. This time it was traffic lights – every set we met was red. My husband, getting agitated at pulling up at yet another set of red lights, said exasperatedly (not expecting an answer):

'Why is it, every set of lights is red?'

After a few seconds Stephanie's small voice piped up: 'I know why traffic lights go red, Daddy.'

Through gritted teeth my husband replied: 'Why, my dear sweet daughter, do traffic lights turn red?'

'So that the drivers can have a rest,' she replied with sweet logic.

*Karen Hilton*

My daughter, aged four, was in the car, being driven to Sunday school when, suddenly, another car driver very foolishly pulled out in front of us.

'Stupid prick,' my daughter yelled out of the open window, just as we arrived at the church door for all to hear.

*Janis Cunningham*

"STUPID PRICK!"

Overheard in a car park yesterday.

Little girl speaking to her mother (who was driving): 'Mummy, on the way home, I want you to sit in the back with me.'

*Joan Ray*

# Grandmas and Grandpas

Our two grandchildren stay overnight on a Saturday while their parents have a free night.

This particular time, about four o'clock in the morning when we were sound asleep, Ffion knocked on the bedroom door, came in, and said:

'Would you flush the toilet, Nanna, because if I do it, it will wake you up.'

*Betty Bowdler*

My grandson Philip, aged two and a half, was strapped safely into his car-seat, on the way to meet Mummy at the station. I climbed into the driving seat and, duly belted up and ready to drive off, selected first gear and asked: 'All right then, Philip?'

Having received an approving (not quite what I had in mind) 'Yes, that's right, Nana', and having been brought up on a diet of *Rawhide* and *Waggon-train*, I then yelled out: 'Right, waggons roll!'

Voice of correction from back seat: 'No, Nanna. Not Waggon. *Sausage*.'

The generation-gap light dawned! Now, we always start our journeys with: 'Sausage Roll.'

*Pearl Hawkins*

While I was sitting in front of the mirror doing my make-up, my granddaughter, Hayley, asked:

'Why do you put that stuff on your face?'

'To make me look beautiful,' I replied.

'When will it start to work?' she asked.

*Lorna Compton*

Like most grandparents I've done my share of childminding. While in the park with Alex, three and a half, a beautiful female went past in a sari, ring through her nose and lots of gold bangles. Alex stared after her and, seeing his interest, I said:

'That's an Indian lady, Alex.'

'Is she a goodie or a baddie?' he turned and whispered.

Another time, while I was looking after his cousin, Carl, aged four, I passed the time of day with a lady in town. Carl tugged me away, saying urgently:

'You *mustn't* speak to strangers, Grandma.'

*Jane Dales*

My four-year-old granddaughter, Katherine, was lying on the carpet next to me as I got on with the ironing.

I became aware that she had turned over on to her back and was looking up my skirt.

'Katherine,' I said crossly, 'what are you doing?'

'Grandma,' she replied indignantly, 'I am trying to see if you have Mickey Mouse on your knickers.'

*Nancy Neocleous*

My son Nigel's little boy is four years old (going on forty!). He often rings me up for a chat and, one day after our telephone conversation, I said:

'Could I have a word with Daddy, please?'

'Yes, Grandma,' he said. 'Hang on.'

Then I heard him call: 'Nige . . . It's your mother.'

*Dorothy Tompsett*

I have a three-year-old, very intelligent with large vocabulary, grandson, Edward, whose one desire in life is to find his way to Windsor Castle without his mother and have tea with the Drum Major. This makes life difficult as he runs off at the drop of a hat.

My daughter was telling me (in front of Edward) that they were going to the airport to meet her husband, and she was dreading a late arrival of his plane because Edward would keep running off.

'Edward,' I said, trying to be helpful, 'if you keep running off and losing Mummy at the airport you will get so scared. There will be so many people that she will never find you. Then you will cry and people will say: "Oh, that little boy is lost, where is his mummy?" Then they will call the policeman and he will say: "Oh, poor little boy, where do you live and where is your mummy?" Everybody will be *so* worried.'

Edward looked at me very seriously for a moment, sighed and, as he walked off, said: 'How ridiculous.'

I felt rather deflated!

*Anne Butler Smith*

Some time ago the family were gathered for coffee and I noticed my grandson David, three plus a bit, constantly tucking into the biscuits without his mum and the rest noticing – they were too busy gossiping.

A bit later I noticed he was rubbing his tummy, so I said conspiratorially:

'Have you got a pain in your tum? That must be all those biscuits you've been sneaking.'

'Nanny,' he replied indignantly, 'I haven't got a tummy-ache. My biscuits have got a headache.'

There's no answer to that, is there?

*Elizabeth Giles*

This would amuse Desmond Morris.

Our granddaughter, aged about four, was standing by my husband's chair. Suddenly, she picked up his hand and said:

'Is this your last skin, Grandpa?'

*Kathleen Mason*

I was shopping with my great-grandson Jordan, aged two and a half, and my daughter-in-law. I left them for a few minutes to buy myself a piece of cod for lunch. On rejoining them the following conversation took place:

Jordan: 'Where have you been?'

Me: 'I bought some fish.'

Jordan (*after slight pause*): 'Have you got a tank?'

Me: 'No, I haven't, Jordan.'

Jordan (*after another pause*): 'I'll buy you one, Nanny June.'

My daughter-in-law and I both had the same vision of a piece of cod fillet floating in a fish tank. We spent five minutes explaining that big fish are for eating, but the pretty ones go into aquariums, like his daddy's, but the dear little chap is still puzzled.

*June Wicks*

Granddad and Nan go to Germany to see their children and grandchildren. Nan, like any district nurse who has a lot of experience with cancer, is violently opposed to smoking. Granddad is trying to give it up. However, he weakens and, with no bolt-hole in Germany, his 'solution' is to take his grandchild, Rachel, to the swings in a nearby park.

On return, Nan, suspicious, asked Rachel: 'Has Granddad been smoking?'

'No,' the child replied. 'But he puts white things in his mouth and then throws them away. That's *very* naughty because we have strict laws on litter in Germany.'

Out of the mouths of babes . . .

*N.N. and C.R. Thomas*

Our dear mam died last year and Cassie (our granddaughter, aged five) was explaining to her little friend:

'We have to take care of our grampa because he's very sad. Our nanna died and we had a *crying* party.'

*Gloria Pay*

We have four grandchildren, the youngest, Gavin, being three years old and going through the finicky food syndrome.

Trying to persuade him to eat his lunch, I said he wouldn't grow curly hair if he didn't eat his veg.

'I'm a little boy,' he replied. 'I'm not a girl. I don't need curly hair.'

Not to be outdone, I said, 'Well, your Daddy's got really lovely curly hair.'

'Yes,' he replied. 'That's 'cos he ate too many vegetables when he was a little boy.'

*Trixie Taylor*

Keri (*aged four*) to his great-grandfather: 'Granddad, how old are you?'

Granddad (*rather proudly*): 'I'm eighty-four.'

Keri: 'Oh, you're *nearly* dead, then.'

*Gloria Pay*

When my daughter Beckie was three years old, she was travelling on a bus to town with her grandmother. In the unselfconscious way that children do, she was kneeling on the seat, facing the other passengers. One particular lady smiled at her and this sparked up a conversation. She asked Beckie her age and her name, and then learnt that Beckie was soon to be a bridesmaid.

By this time, several other people were taking an interest and Beckie, triumphant, suddenly exclaimed:

'My nannie can take her teeth out.'

My poor mother still relates this story. Beckie is now twenty-seven, and soon to be married.

*Pat Newman*

Marcus, aged four (very much into numbers, especially ages of people), said to Shirley:

'Nan, I'm four, aren't I? And Jamie and Arron are two, aren't they? Mummy is thirty-three – a three and a three. But Nan, how much are you?'

Shirley: 'I'm fifty-eight, Marcus – a five and an eight.'

Marcus: '*Christ*!' (One of his father's expletives.)

On another occasion, Marcus, meeting his cousin Arron's other gran, was told:

'Her name is Rose.'

He turned to his grandmother, Shirley, and remarked:

'Well, *I* think she looks more like a daffodil *actually*.'

*Shirley and John Dyde*

I am a fairly fit 54-year-old, and need to be as my grandchildren Carl and Amy are nearly four and two and a half.

At Christmas, a very ancient crib scene comes out, complete with Mary, Joseph, kings, shepherds and baby Jesus, all made by my sons Blue Peter-fashion out of loo rolls, etc.

Amy especially loved baby Jesus and each time she went into the lounge she picked Him up, gave Him a kiss, and put Him back into the manger.

After Christmas she went into the lounge and stopped dead. 'Oh,' she said, 'baby Jesus gone!'

I explained that, now that Christmas was over, I had packed everything carefully away.

'Where?' asked Amy.

'In the loft ready for next year,' I answered.

'Oh, right,' she said, trotting away.

While this conversation was going on Carl was looking at several photos, grouped together in a large frame.

'Who's that, Nan?' he asked.

I told him and so it continued right through all the photos, until he came to one of my husband.

'And who's that, Nan?'

'That's Granddad Irvine, darling,' I replied.

'Where is he, Nan?'

'He died when you were a baby.'

'Where is he now, Nan?'

'He has gone to heaven to live with Jesus.'

He paused, then added:

'Is he in the loft, Nan?'

I know I put a great many things in the loft, but . . .

*Patricia Irvine*

My grandson Michael is now ten, but, when he first started school, Mummy asked him on his return home what he had had for school dinner.

'Wind in the Willow Hole,' he replied.

After a few more questions, it turned out that he had had 'Toad in the Hole'.

Well, he was almost right!

*Doreen Ralph*

Our granddaughter Amy, aged five, would like to be a hairdresser (so she says) and practises on me.

The other afternoon she was busy combing my hair and was unusually quiet for a very long time. After a time her head peered round from behind me, and she said reassuringly:

'It's all right, Granny, I'm just looking for nits.'

Needless to say, I was in the clear!

*Anthea Brownjohn*

When our granddaughter Heather was two and three-quarters, she had had her bath and was 'reading' a book to Grandpa. I came in with her beaker of warmed milk, and said to her:

'If you hold that little book in one hand, you can hold your beaker in the other hand.'

With that, she put her book down, held out both her hands and said:

'Grandma, you know I've only got *two* pairs of hands.'

*Miair Hudson*

My grandson Scott wanted to go to the loo in a large department store. My daughter Jackie took him to a ladies' and on their way out they saw a gentleman going into the men's loo. My grandson looked at him and, in a very loud voice, said:

'Are you going in there for a wee-wee?'

The bemused man replied yes, he was going for a wee-wee, whereupon my grandson said:

'Well, *don't* forget to wash your hands.'

The man nearly collapsed with laughter, and my daughter with embarrassment. Hey ho!

*Kathy Woodall*

My five-year-old granddaughter, Zoe, loves dinosaurs, and is forever pestering Mummy with questions about them. This is the latest:

'Mummy, how many people do dinosaurs eat every day?'

'I don't know, Zoe, they lived a million years ago.'

'Was that when Grandma was a little girl?'

*E. Hellewell*

I suggested that my three-year-old granddaughter should make a card for Grampy for when he returned from Australia.

'What will it say?' I asked (meaning, of course, the words inside).

'*Silly* Granny,' she replied. 'Cards don't talk.'

*Rosealeen Lane*

When putting flowers on Grandma's grave, my young son asked:

'Do you fink she can see the flowers?'

'I shouldn't really think so,' I said.

'Perhaps she can just see the stalks,' he replied.

*Audrey of Beccles*

We took our four-year-old grandson, Joseph, to the 'Teddy Bears' Concert' at the Barbican.

He enjoyed the afternoon, joining in the sing-alongs, and, at various times, went to the loo with either me or grandpa.

On return home, his mummy asked, 'What was the best part of the concert, Joseph?'

Without a moment's hesitation, he replied, 'Going to the toilet with Grandpa.'

*Rosalind Harris*

My grandson Matthew, at about two and a half years old, was playing happily in the garden in his sandpit. Mummy was upstairs making the beds.

'Mummy,' Matthew called up. 'It's cold outside. Can I come and play indoors?'

'Of course you can, darling,' Mummy said. 'I will be down soon and we will have lunch.'

Some time later Mummy came downstairs, and put her head round the lounge door. There, in the middle of her BRAND NEW carpet, was Matthew playing with his sandpit!

He had filled his toy wheelbarrow with sand, obviously making several trips to and from the garden, and was quite happily making sandpies, etc.

'Hallo, Mummy,' he smiled sweetly!

*Doreen Wilkinson*

Two-year-old James visits Great Granny with his mother and sisters. They are all given lemonade in safely heavy glasses. James takes his and, rushing at his sister, slams his glass against hers, yelling: 'Cheers.' Then, turning to Great Granny, adds: 'When do the pubs open?'

As no one in the family frequents a pub we are all flabbergasted.

*Margaret Young*

When they lived in Norfolk, I used to visit my family, including grandson Andrew, frequently. It gave him great pleasure to come into my bed at the crack of dawn, armed with his dressing-gown cord and a wicked grin. The next thing, he would get under the duvet and tie my legs firmly together (delightful when you are more than half asleep).

On asking why he treated his poor old Gran in *such* a way, he answered:

'Because I like you.'

*Norah Smith*

When my grandson was about three, his mother had friends in for coffee. I arrived, newly permed, and he watched me warily for a while with a puzzled look on his face. Then, suddenly, he said:

'Are you Nana?'

After we had all finished laughing, he was so relieved to discover that I was indeed Nana.

He is now fifteen, and a few days ago he gave me a hug and said:

'You always smell like Christmas.'

*Gaye Young*

I was telling Andrew, aged four, that his granny would be looking after him for a while as I was going into hospital for an operation (a hysterectomy) as I had a problem with my tummy. As he had very recently been presented with a baby brother he obviously felt very knowledgeable about such things.

'Oh yes,' he said knowingly, 'you will go into hospital, get into bed, and out of your tummy will come a baby, and then your problem will be *gone*.' (Upturned hands to emphasize this.)

I wonder if he will be of the same opinion in a few months' time, when his baby brother is still around – *and crawling.*

*Linda Baldwin*

My daughter-in-law was telling her three young children that it was my mother's birthday.

'How old is she?' asked seven-year-old Edward.

'Ninety-one,' she replied.

'And is she *alive*?' the flabbergasted child asked.

*Anon*

I had my two grandchildren staying with me, and having put them to bed, I staggered downstairs to put my feet up.

A few minutes later I heard Sarah crying, and went up to ask her what was the matter.

'I am frightened, Granny,' she said.

When I asked why, my grandson said:

'I'm not frightened of anything, Granny.'

Then, after a long pause, he continued:

'Except for the dinosaurs and witches that came through your window.'

You can imagine the effect this had on Sarah!

*Betty Atkins*

My grandson Oliver, when aged four and a half, came to stay a few days. We had been talking about his two grandfathers (both of whom passed away the year he was born). You know the patter:

'She's *not* coming yet, Jesus.'

*Dot Fox*

I had my two grandchildren staying with me, and having put them to bed, I staggered downstairs to put my feet up.

A few minutes later I heard Sarah crying, and went up to ask her what was the matter.

'I am frightened, Granny,' she said.

When I asked why, my grandson said:

'I'm not frightened of anything, Granny.'

Then, after a long pause, he continued:

'Except for the dinosaurs and witches that came through your window.'

You can imagine the effect this had on Sarah!

*Betty Atkins*

We were visiting our daughter's home, and our granddaughter Emma, aged two, had a cold and the usual runny nose. I got a tissue and said:

'Come on, Emma, let's blow your nose.'

'It's all right, Grandma,' came the serious, straight-faced reply, 'I've got my sleeve.'

*June Simmons*

My great-grandson (I've got four of 'em) had come over from Woking with my daughter and family to take me to spend the day with them. As we were driving along, he said:

'Nanny, do you drive?'

'No, dear.'

'Why not?'

'I haven't got a car.'

'You *could* buy one.'

'Not much good really, I'm too old now.'

He studied me a moment and said:

'Nanny, you are not old, you are *lovely*.'

Talk about beauty being in the eye of the beholder. He was seven then (eight now) and I was seventy-nine (now eighty).

*Lily Cox*

Our son brought his girlfriend and her four-year-old, Marcus, to stay for a few days. We hadn't met before, so, to put Marcus at ease, I bought him a water jet pistol. On arrival, he excitedly went out to play in the garden, but was obviously minus a playmate to fire at. To compensate for this, I filled my plant spray with water and we squirted each other for ten minutes, hiding behind shed, greenhouse and so on. By then, I was absolutely soaking so I came indoors to change.

Marcus, missing me, came into the kitchen, and said to my husband:

'Where's that girl gone?'

'What girl?' my husband replied, puzzled.

'*Your* girl,' Marcus replied.

As a fifty-seven-year-old grandmother I was very flattered, and young Marcus is now a most welcome guest!

*Delyse Upton*

My grandson burst through my front door yesterday, saying:

'When I am eight, I am not going to cuddle you any more, Granny.'

'Oh, darling,' I replied, 'how *very* disappointing – I am upset.'

Whereupon he looked thoughtful and added:

'Well, maybe I'll wait to stop until I am sixty-one.'

*Betty Atkins*

My grandson Luke, aged five, was sitting in the kitchen one day playing with my lettuce-spinner.

'Don't break it, dear,' I said, 'I often use it to spin my pants in . . .'

At which, as he took one look at the size of my bottom, we both roared with laughter.

But when I went to his 'open day' at school and read his 'newsletter', the laugh, I'm afraid, was on me.

He had written, 'My grandma spins her pants in the lettuce spinner. I don't know how she gets them in, they're such a size . . .'

Nice, eh. Who wants grandchildren?

*Ruth Watson*

At my age, my hair is a mixture of white, black and grey. One day my granddaughter looked up into my face and said, 'I don't know what colour your hair is, Nana, but I don't like it.'

*Beryl Gawthorne*

Granddad spent absolutely ages fitting some stabilizers to our granddaughter Katy's first two-wheeler.

She jumped on the bike, pedalled once up and down the cul-de-sac, came back, and said, 'Right, Granddad, I've got the hang of it. You can take them off again.'

*Irene Cain*

Four-year-old James asked his great-grandmother Irma, a member of our day centre:

'Nana, can you swim?'

Nana: 'No, I can't, James.'

James: 'Don't worry – I'll teach you when you get a bit older.'

He could not understand why we all fell about laughing!

*Ann Dunkley* (Trinity Hospice)

My husband Eric and I have been taking aid lorries to Romania for four years now and, since the summer of 1991, our young granddaughter, Jennifer, has accompanied us. Having her travel three thousand miles in the back of the cab of a seventeen-tonne truck on three of our summer journeys to Arad has been very special for us. During those three years, of course, she came out with many gems, but none to better the one in 1992 when she was coming up to five.

Just before we left for Romania that August, I learnt that two days after we got back I would have to go into hospital for a hysterectomy. As a neighbour of Jennifer's had just died from cancer of the stomach, she was very worried about Granny going into hospital, and I reassured her that Granny was not going to die, in fact Granny would be fine. No more was said about the impending 'op' until we were on our way home from Romania having breakfast in a German motorway café. Then, out of the blue, she said:

'You're not going to die, are you, Granny?'

I reassured her again that, no, of course, Granny wasn't going to die. She then lowered her head and, in a very grown-up voice, said:

'Now, Granny, you do realize that this means you can't have any more children, don't you?' Adding: 'But it doesn't matter, Granny, 'cos now you're *my* Granny you don't need to be a mum any more anyway.'

*Ann Long*

My daughter Sarah, aged four, visited Granny the day following the Trooping the Colour ceremony. Gran asked her if she had watched the Queen Trooping the Colour.

'Is that when the Queen wears a red coat, and black skirt, and a black hat, and sits on a horse?' Sarah asked warily.

'Yes, that's right, dear,' Gran replied.

Sarah, *very* pleased with herself:

'Yes, that's her birthday suit, Granny.'

*Eileen Knight*

My granddaughter Poppy, then aged six, was recalling her first visit to London from her home in Torquay with her Granny. Of the things she had seen (and remembered) was:

'Talking to the hamburger men at the Tower of London.'

What would the Beefeaters say!

*Clive Kingcome*

My elder son, Donald, who is now a most respected and upright member of the teaching profession, went to stay with his Nanny and Grandad when he was about two and a half. Upon returning from a walk with his grandfather, my mother noticed the signs of chocolate around his lips and remarked to young Donald:

'Your Grandad's been spoiling you.'

To which Donald replied, with great dignity:

'Yes, isn't he a kind old bugger?'

*Martin KcKenna*

Some years ago, when my grandchildren were over here from America, I took them to see the plaque placed near to Deal Castle recording the landing on the nearby beach of Julius Caesar in the year 55 BC.

My grandson – then aged about four and a half – turned to me and said, 'Were you living here then, Nanna?'

*Esme Mackins*

JULIUS
CAESAR
LANDED
HERE IN
55 BC

## Schoolies

Being an only child was a wonderful experience for me and, in our house, listening to music was a major activity. Mum (the beatific Norma) enjoyed Country and Western; Dad (the beatific Edward) enjoyed classical, especially Wagner. All those tales of Brunhild and Valkyrie excited me no end.

When I was five and just getting to grips with school, the teacher came upon me playing and asked me what I was doing. Being an imaginative child I said:

'I am Brunhild collecting the souls of the dead that have fallen in battle.'

Before she could close her mouth, my stubby little legs carried me off round the playground.

*Joy Young*

Our son Malcolm, when he was about five, used to dash in from primary school at three-thirty and eagerly turn on the television to watch the children's programmes. One day he came back out of the lounge, looking very downcast, and said:

'Mummy, there's a programme on the television and I don't like it. It's called "The Budget".'

The powers-that-be had replaced his programmes with 'politics'!

*Elizabeth Battin*

My son Andrew (now thirty-eight and the father of James and Lucy) had heard us talking about my father having been to the opening of the new terminal building at Manchester airport. When we went to Andrew's Open Day, there in his 'News' book he had written:

'My grandpa went to Manchester Airport and met the Duke of Edinburgh and some other impotent men.'

*Dorothy Bisatt*

Steve was born prematurely and suffered a few physical disadvantages. As a consequence we were advised to send him to a special school from the age of three.

Despite his physical disadvantages, Steve has a wonderful sense of humour and his granddad was in the habit of telling him risqué jokes.

Having spent the weekend with his grandparents Steve was full of fun on the Monday, and all went well until lunch, when it was the practice for the teacher to eat with the children.

With the children duly settled, it was the teachers' turn to help themselves to food. Steve's teacher, Sue Martin, duly returned with a large helping of beans. Whereupon Steven burst out laughing and said:

'My granddad calls them shirt-lifters.'

*Sue and Alan Fuller*

Carl was at primary school and had been asked to write all about 'My Mummy'.

Carl: 'Mum, what do you do at work?'

Me (*I worked in a hairdresser's*): 'Oh, everything, dear, wash up, sweep up hair, pick up wet towels. I'm just a dogsbody, really.'

So, Carl wrote: 'My mummy goes to work and she is a dog's body. My daddy is a pleese man (policeman).'

My best friend's son, Andrew, wrote: 'My mummy dyes her hair blonde and goes out at night.'

My friend worked nights at an old folk's home. She also had highlights put in her hair!

*Sue Potter*

Richard, aged six, is in a class of twenty-three pupils, and he told them that his father is a farmer (actually he is a draughtsman).

'Is he an arable farmer?' the teacher asked.

'No,' replied Richard. 'He's a *very* nice farmer.'

He then got quite carried away, adding that his father bred horses and it just so happened that twenty-two foals had been born and each classmate was promised one.

Then, just before last Christmas, Richard's mother received an urgent message from the teacher that Richard must be collected immediately because he was suffering from a blinding headache. Even though she was due to collect him shortly (it was almost the end of the day) the teacher insisted that she should come at once. On her arrival, the teacher explained that Richard had not brought his glasses to school and that the eyestrain must have brought on the headache.

'But he doesn't *wear* glasses,' his mother protested.

'Well,' the teacher replied, astonished, 'he has been wearing them all this term.'

Apparently, the glasses had belonged to a grandparent, and Richard had taken them from a desk drawer, and nobody had missed them.

I am sure that, in thirty or forty years' time, Richard will either be selling second-hand cars or running a privatized industry.

*Bob Harrison*

When my daughter was five I had a foster son only a few months younger, and they were in the same class at school. When I fetched them one night, I was told Alan had been fighting in class, so I tried to find out why. Alan was recounting a long, complicated story about someone taking his Lego when Samantha suddenly interrupted *very* firmly and said:

'Yes, but there was no need to fight about it *in public*!'

The emphasis on the last two words would have done credit to any social-climbing adult. All these years later she's grown to a beautiful young woman who still cares very much what people think.

*Philippa Settle*

My granddaughter Natallie was six years old when her school class was told that Sarah's daddy had had a heart attack the previous evening and had been taken to hospital for resuscitation.

This information was relayed to us with all the drama that a six-year-old can muster.

'Sarah's daddy,' she said, 'had a broken heart last night and they took him to hospital to suffocate him.'

Another day, Natallie, still aged six, and I were sitting on the plinth of a display model in Marks & Spencer waiting for my wife and daughter to finish shopping. I noticed Natallie's lower lip jutting out, and asked what was the matter.

'Granddad,' she replied, 'shopping is boring, expensive and bad for your health.'

*Gordon Smith*

Several years ago I worked as a school secretary in a village primary school. We had a trio of brothers who, like many of the children, were transported in from outlying villages. All had exceptionally healthy appetites, especially the youngest who, even his mother admitted, was not quite 'the full load', and he was teased unmercifully at home and school by his two brothers.

They always came to school well stoked after a hearty breakfast, each carrying a luncheon box packed to the gunnels with sandwiches and so on, plus a few pence to spend at the tuck shop.

One morning the youngest didn't arrive and, just before lunch, I received a telephone call from his mother saying that she had been up all night with this child because of 'toilet problems'. She went on to say that, after much probing, the problem was found to lie smack at the door of his brothers, who had fed him laxative chocolate (almost a whole bar) on the homeward bus the previous afternoon!

'It's probably done us a favour,' she added. 'You know what a sweet freak he is.'

Sure enough when he re-appeared the next day looking not his usual robust self he was heard to say:

'I've gorn orff chocolate a bit.'

As a school secretary, I could fill a book on children's antics that have to be experienced to be believed. Like the youngster who had an 'accident' in the classroom one afternoon. Fearing the worst from his mother he secretly emptied the contents of his pants down the back of the central-heating pipes. The pipes, of course, went all around the walls and were blazing away because it was winter! Fortunately, it was a small school and everyone was evacuated under the 'cover' of a fire drill while the offending material was found and dealt with.

*Anon*

When my granddaughter Sophia, four and a half, had just started school she came on a visit, and announced proudly:

'Grandma, I'm going on a trip with school to see some birds and butterflies and animals.'

'That's nice, darling,' I said. 'Are you going on a bus?'

With hands on hips, she said indignantly:

'Grandma! I've just told you. I'm *not* going on a bus. I'm going on a *trip*.'

*Pauline Bennett*

My granddaughter Bethany was sick in bed during the night and her mother was telling her that if she didn't feel well at school to make sure she told the teacher, and, if she was very unwell, she would be able to come home.

'Oh,' said Bethany, 'if you're not well at school you don't come home – you just put your head in a bucket.'

*D. Minors*

At the local flower club the demonstrator was telling us that her granddaughter had recently started school and that the child's mother was worried about the school lunches, because the child was a 'bit fussy' about what she ate.

On collecting the child on the first day, the mother immediately asked her what she had had for lunch.

'Oh! It was nice,' the child replied. 'We had three choices. Fish, salad or meat in tea bags.'

It was ravioli!

*Patricia Turner*

My mother-in-law, Dorothy, tells this story about the time when she was a primary-school teacher.

There was great excitement in the classroom because one of the little boys was impatiently awaiting the arrival of a new little brother or sister.

One morning, he rushed into the class and announced proudly: 'I've got a new baby brother!'

'That's nice, George,' my mother-in-law said. 'What are you going to call him?'

'Spot,' he replied.

'Surely not. Spot isn't a little boy's name, is it, George?'

George was very quiet for the rest of the morning, then, returning to school after lunch, informed everyone:

'His name is *not* Spot . . . it is Mark. I knew it was something to do with a stain.'

*Pat Nicholls*

I am blind, with a guide dog, and go round all the local schools speaking about the training of dogs. Jasmin is my sixth guide dog so I have many stories: some funny, some sad, but the children love them all.

A couple of years ago I was talking at an infant school and, at question time, a little boy put up his hand.

'Miss, you can't be blind, your eyes are open.'

I explained that most blind people have their eyes open, but the eyes just don't work. Then I added: 'But these eyes aren't real. Some years ago I had a very serious operation, and these eyes are plastic.'

He sat down for a while, thinking, then his hand shot up again.

'Yes, Gary,' the teacher said, 'what would you like to ask Mrs Hill now?'

'Go on, take 'em out and show us,' said Gary triumphantly.

Follow that!

*Kathy Hill*

My mother, staying with my family in Scotland for a couple of weeks, said to our number-one daughter (three-ish) who was looking very thoughtful:

'Good morning, Kirsteen, and how are you this morning?'

'Very well, thank you, Grandma,' Kirsteen replied politely, 'but it's starting to rain and I've just cleaned my *bloody* windows.'

We never discovered where she learned that expression – but think it must have been at Sunday school!

*John Tarbotton*

My daughter Carole is a staff nurse, and her son Adam, aged nineteen months, goes to the hospital crèche. The 'age-stages' of the various groups are: babies, tiddlers, toddlers, littlies and biggies. Adam had graduated to the toddlers and his group had been playing in the home section. When Carole collected him, his keyworker Dayan (pronounced Diane) said tongue-in-cheek:

'Perhaps you had better have a word with your son re his cooking. He made pretend-buns today, put them in the "oven" and then climbed in after them!'

*Jackie Atkinson*

My niece, when a small girl, came home from school with a lot of coppers in her pocket. When her mother asked where she had got them all from, her answer was that she had charged threepence a bite from the big apple her mother had given her.

She now holds down a responsible position in a bank.

*Charles Barton*

The following poem, 'My Dad's Unsuccessful Race', was written by Danuel, aged eight:

> My dad went to run in a race
> He ran at quite an unsteady pace
> The look on his face was red and mean
> He looked just like a big sunbeam
> My Dad got to the end of the track
> But then he fell over
> Splat! on his back.

Well, at least it rhymes!

*Su Hillman*

Alice (now eleven) was asking me to help her with her biology revision:

'Can you,' she said, 'show me where the ribs are attached to the scrotum?'

Sounds jolly painful – glad I'm not a man.

*Geraldine Bennett*

Everybody was quiet, having been told to stop talking. One child then spoke to his silent companion.

When asked why he was *still* talking, he answered: 'I wasn't talking, Sir, I was just telling him not to.'

*Jean*

# ACKNOWLEDGEMENTS

*Special thanks are due to the following people who have freely and very generously donated contributions to this book to support BBC Children in Need:*

**Contributors to** Sarah Kennedy's BBC Radio Two programme who have given permission for their letters to be included in this book. Every effort has been made by Sarah Kennedy and BBC Books to contact contributors. Should they have failed to do so, they will be pleased to correct this, after notification, at the earliest opportunity.

**Cartoonists**

Barry Appleby, Neil Bennett, Simon Bond, Chris Burke, Clive Collins, Frank Dickens, Maurice Dodd, Dorrien, Hunt Emerson, Haro, Jim Hutchings, Kathryn Lamb, Larry, Mac, Sue Macartney-Snape, Peter Maddocks, Matt, Bill Mevin, Geo Parkin, Ken Pyne, Posy Simmonds, Trog.

Paul Gravett, The National Museum of Cartoon Art, 'Carriage Row', 183 Eversholt Street, London NW1 1DD